Family Conflict

Family Conflict

Heather E. Canary and Daniel J. Canary

polity

4-2-14
LN
$ 22.95

First published in 2013 by Polity Press

Polity Press
65 Bridge Street
Cambridge CB2 1UR, UK

Polity Press
350 Main Street
Malden, MA 02148, USA

ISBN-13: 978-0-7456-4660-2
ISBN-13: 978-0-7456-4661-9(pb)

A catalogue record for this book is available from the British Library.

Typeset in 11 on 13 pt Sabon
by Servis Filmsetting Ltd, Stockport, Cheshire
Printed and bound in Great Britain by Clays Ltd, St Ives PLC

The publisher has used its best endeavours to ensure that the URLs for external websites referred to in this book are correct and active at the time of going to press. However, the publisher has no responsibility for the websites and can make no guarantee that a site will remain live or that the content is or will remain appropriate.

Every effort has been made to trace all copyright holders, but if any have been inadvertently overlooked the publisher will be pleased to include any necessary credits in any subsequent reprint or edition.

For further information on Polity, visit our website: www.politybooks.com

We dedicate this book to our siblings, who gave us our earliest lessons in family conflict:

Holly Chase and Jon Bucher

David Canary, Richard Canary, and Debby Tankersley

Contents

Detailed Contents

Tables and Figures

Preface

This book concerns the contexts and content of family conflict. In the past 30 years, scholars have spent enormous energy and talent exploring the nature and processes of family conflict. This book likewise emphasizes the nature of family conflict with an eye on elaborating processes involved. More precisely, we provide background information that is necessary for understanding how family members use communication behaviors to manage their conflicts.

A multi-level model of family conflict helps to unify what we offer. That model is elaborated in chapter 1. For now, however, we should indicate its primary features, which are interconnected. At Level 4, culture occupies the highest, most abstract level containing other family conflict issues. Level 3 entails four structural factors that affect all family members: family status (e.g., intact vs. divorced homes), work–life integration, health of family members, and resiliency of the family to cope with difficulties. Level 2 regards relational-level processes that focus on marital, interparental, parent–child, and sibling relationships. Finally, Level 1 concerns the individual's experiences with conflict, including factors such as personal development, cognitive reactions, and personality. Each of these levels is represented in this book to the extent that the research takes us there.

Several themes emerge in this book. First, the research reflects that family conflict is inevitable. As Shantz and Hartup (1992) observed, "Conflicts – between people and within people – are part and parcel of everyday living, and to such an extent that they must be regarded as intrinsic to the human condition" (p. 1). Of course, the inevitability of family conflict applies to everyone, though the frequency with which conflict occurs varies according to the external and internal pressures on family members, how they prefer to manage conflict, and whether or not the conflict is resolved.

The second theme concerns how family conflict management can be constructive or destructive (Deutsch, 1973). This theme reflects a strong current in the research literature. Putnam (2006) summarized the functional and dysfunctional aspects of conflict. Functional conflict can prevent system stagnation, stimulate interest, promote cohesiveness in groups, help lead to change, and so forth. Dysfunctional conflict can harm relationships, lead to intractable stalemates, foster entrenched behaviors, and the like. However, much of the research emphasizes the negative features of conflict, for example, how intense, chronic, and unresolved it might be. One can find this reliance on the negative (to the exclusion of positive) in research on interparental conflict, adolescent sibling conflict, and elsewhere.

Third, family conflict operates very differently in different types of family relationships. Marital conflict looks very different than parent–child conflict, which looks very different than sibling conflict. Although these relational contexts overlap and permeate each other, they remain distinct and house sometimes qualitatively different forms of conflict.

Fourth, and related to the point above, families assume different types. For example, Koerner and Fitzpatrick (2006) present four alternative types of families: consensual, pluralistic, protective, and laissez-faire. These types are discussed in chapter 1. In addition, we discuss differences in marriage types, stepfamily types, single-parent family types, and sibling types.

Finally, the research yields many implications regarding family conflict. Many facts regarding family conflict can be variously unexpected, and we extend these to reflect on how readers might anticipate what is unexpected to become knowledgeable about their own family conflict experiences. Importantly as well, learning what to expect will offer ideas about how to anticipate and manage family conflict when it arises. In this light, we conclude each chapter with a section titled "Implications."

There are a few issues that we do not emphasize. First, it is impossible to cover all topics that might be relevant to family conflict. Entire books have been written on each of the chapters (e.g., Cummings & Davies, 2010). For instance, we do not cover research on psychological, physical, and sexual abuse. Similarly, we do not cover hurtful messages, dominance, or compliance-gaining tactics. These domains of behavior remain important in their own right, of course. Accordingly, and out of survival necessity, we selected what we consider the most important material to review. Second, we do not discuss particular contexts related to family conflict (largely due to a lack of empirical evidence regarding them). These include cohabiting couples, same-sex partnerships, extended family members, parents and adopted children, and so forth.

We hope that the reader finds this book both interesting and informative. We begin each chapter with a story that foreshadows a segment of the chapter. We have based these on actual events, so these stories should sound realistic and plausible. As further resources, we have included two appendices at the back of the book. Appendix 1 contains discussion questions for each chapter. These discussion questions invite students to answer a question and provide a rationale for their answers. Most often, these discussion questions require a reading of the book. Appendix 2 contains media examples (i.e., films that help illustrate the chapter themes). In addition to a quick summary of the plot, we provide the date, actors, and ratings of the films. We hope that these features will add to the reader's appreciation of the principles and findings in this book. We encourage the reader to use our discussions, resources, and references as starting points for deeper explorations of topics they find particularly compelling.

Finally, we wish to thank several people who helped make this book possible. The editors at Polity Press, Andrea Drugan and Lauren Mulholland, were extremely helpful, encouraging, and patient as we experienced delays and re-imaginings during the project. We appreciate the hard work of the production staff at Polity Press, including Ian Tuttle and Neil de Cort, who corrected our mistakes and shaped our manuscript into a finished product. Also, we thank our families for encouraging and teasing us along the way.

1

Introduction to Family Conflict

Adam grabbed a shovel to plant the roses he had just purchased. He was looking forward to time bonding with his 14-year-old stepson, Bryson. He imagined them planting the roses together. Stopping at Bryson's room he announced, "For this weekend's chore, you are going to help me plant these roses." Bryson was irritated but followed Adam outside. Once outside, Adam handed him the shovel and pointed to circles he had drawn on the ground. "OK, we need to start by shoveling holes in the ground." But instead of shoveling, Bryson protested, "Why don't you get a gardener?" "I can't afford a gardener," Adam replied. "Why don't you make Mark (his older brother) do this? This isn't fair." Adam reacted, "Look, this is your only chore for the weekend and if you stop whining and do it, you will finish before noon." Bryson replied, "I don't want to; give me something else to do."

We all have experienced various forms of conflict in our families, some leading to constructive outcomes and some leading to destructive outcomes. This book focuses on family conflict and how the reader can help their family conflicts lead to more constructive outcomes.

We begin by discussing why this book is warranted. That is, why should we study family conflict? Then we define *family* and *conflict*. Third, relevant theoretic approaches are illustrated. Theory is critical for understanding family conflict. Next, we present a model that summarizes key features of family conflict. Finally, we offer a preview of the remaining chapters in this book.

The Importance of Family Conflict

Many reasons exist to study family conflict. Knowing that conflict is an unexpected occurrence for family members represents the first reason to examine family conflict. The reader can learn about unexpected processes in conflict in order to anticipate them. Sillars and Weisberg (1987) noted that conflicts tend to be confusing and surprising, although interpersonal conflicts are natural to the human condition. That is, conflicts most typically occur when people are doing something else, such as having dinner, driving in the car, doing homework, or walking the dog. So we are often caught off guard by conflicts (which are also part of our own making).

Second, how conflict is managed has direct implications for the quality of family relationships. Consider the marriage relationship. As Gottman (1994) observed, "Nearly all the research on marital interaction has involved the observation of conflict resolution" (p. 66). And this research shows that the destructive use of conflict messages more so than constructive use of messages predicts both the quality of the marriage as well as divorce (Kelley, 2012).

Third, family members are affected by how conflict is managed psychologically as well as socially. One of the clearest findings in the interparental and parent–child conflict research is that children become more withdrawn to the extent their parents use negative communication tactics. Moreover, parents sometimes attempt to enlist the help of the child to combat the other parent – a strategy known as "triangulation," which is detrimental to the child as well as the parent–child relationship (e.g., Atkinson et al., 2009).

Next, and related to the point above, how people manage family conflicts can affect their physical health. Both over-expression of anger and avoidance can lead to cardiovascular, endocrine, and immunological system problems (Kiecolt-Glaser & Newton, 2001). In considering the cardiovascular system alone, the use of anger has been found to predict heart disease, high blood pressure, and heart attacks (e.g., Metz & Epstein, 2002; Suarez, 2004). Learning how to cope better with unexpected family conflicts can lead to living longer.

Finally, conflict management occurs within an entire system of family members. Each member influences the others and is influenced by the others. The interrelationships of family members cannot be underestimated. For example, the parent–child conflict literature indicates that the manner in which parents manage conflicts with one child affects how a sibling interprets the relevance of those conflicts for himself/herself (Selman, 1980). Likewise, a reciprocal relationship exists between family members, such that the interplay of conflict communication behaviors must be understood to appreciate how family relationships operate.

No doubt, the reader can think of other reasons as well. And research suggests additional reasons for examining interpersonal conflict (e.g., Canary & Lakey (with Marmo), 2013; Cupach et al., 2010). From what we have outlined here, though, the reader can ascertain why the examination of family conflict is both relevant and important.

Defining Family Conflict

At this juncture, we should define *family conflict*. We do so by first separating these terms and then bringing them back together.

What is a Family?

Defining *family* is not a simple task. Researchers, politicians, healthcare providers, and the average person walking down the street can all have different ideas about what *family* means. One way to arrive at a working definition for this book is to consider criteria that have been used to define what constitutes a family. Segrin and Flora (2005) point to structure, function, and interaction as three criteria for determining who counts as and acts as family. Some definitions focus on structure, or the family *form*, to determine whether a social group is a family or not. For example, the US Census Bureau (2012) states, "A family is a group of two people or more (one of whom is the householder) related by birth, marriage, or adoption and residing together." This definition emphasizes the number of people, a legal relationship, and sharing living space. This definition is useful for eliminating other types of residential social groups, such as fraternity or sorority houses, from the definition of a family.

Another dimension for defining families is function, which refers to the "tasks performed and expected" by those who are considered family (Segrin & Flora, 2005, p. 5). For instance, Patterson (2002) reviewed several functions that researchers and policymakers have identified as primary functions of families: (1) membership and family formation (e.g., providing a sense of belonging); (2) economic support (e.g., providing food and shelter); (3) nurturance, education, and socialization (e.g., instilling social values); and (4) protection of vulnerable members (e.g., protecting young, sick, or otherwise vulnerable members). Using these functions as criteria, any group of people that fulfills these familial functions would be defined as a family, whether they were related by blood, legal bonds, or something else. This dimension is useful for including non-traditional relationships as families that might not be included in a structural definition, such as same-sex couples living with or without their biological children.

The final dimension that has been used to define families highlights interaction, which focuses on ways communication processes constitute family (Segrin & Flora, 2005). As one might expect, communication researchers have been particularly prone to use interaction to define family. For example, Baxter and Braithwaite (2006) focus on this dimension in their definition of family as "a social group of two or more persons, characterized by ongoing interdependence with long-term commitments that stem from blood, law, or affection" (p. 3). This definition downplays structure and function (although those dimensions are still present) as it highlights the importance of interdependence, commitment, and affection for defining who counts as a family.

Our choice of chapter titles indicates some of our own definitional commitments. We offer here a working definition of family that acknowledges the importance of structure, function, and interaction for determining a family. Importantly, we do not offer this working definition as superior to or a substitute for the many valid definitions offered by others. Rather, we offer this simply so the reader knows our position. We define family as "*a long-term group of two or more people related through biological, legal, or equivalent ties and who enact those ties through ongoing interaction providing instrumental and/or emotional support.*"

What is Conflict?

Conflict can be defined in numerous ways (Putnam, 2006). Putnam highlighted the various definitions and also pointed to dimensions that can be used to typify definitions of conflict. Two dimensions of definitions are especially salient to family conflict (Canary et al., 1995). These concern whether conflict occurs in specific behaviors or that behaviors are not necessary to locate conflict. The second dimension regards whether conflicts occur outside of any recognizable episode or are tied to specific episodes that have a clear beginning, middle, and end.

The combination of these two dimensions yields four possible definitions of conflict. The first definition sees conflict as behaviorally specific but free of specific episodes, meaning *conflict is pervasive* in nature. For example, Sprey (1971) held that "the family process *per se* is conceived of as a continuous confrontation between participants with conflicting – though not necessarily opposing – interests in their shared fate" (p. 722). In a congruent manner, Deutsch (1973) defined conflict as any incompatibility between people.

The second definition holds that conflict occurs when particular types of behaviors occur, regardless of hostility. Research on parent–toddler conflict contains such a definition, for example, as two consecutive opposing statements by the mother and child. Accordingly, the number of conflicts in any interaction can be counted by the number of opposing statements. In an academic sense, *conflict is linguistically defined* (as we see in chapter 4).

The third approach emphasizes that conflict represents any episode that is marked by opposition and hostility. In this vein, conflict relies on partners' perceptions of the event as to whether or not it is a conflict. Other terms that represent this definition involve having an "argument," a "quarrel," a "significant disagreement," and so forth. The point is that some scholars see conflict as contained within specific episodes that are typically marked by opposition and hostility. In brief, *conflict is a type of episode.*

Finally, the fourth definition holds that conflict is defined in particular kinds of behaviors enacted within particular kinds of episodes (marked by opposition and hostility). As we can see in the next chapter on marital conflict, researchers have identified specific conflict strategies and tactics that occur in conflict episodes. Here, then, the hallmarks of this definition imply that *conflicts refer to particular episodes containing particular behaviors.*

We refer to conflict as *any incompatibility that can be expressed between people* (Canary & Lakey (with Marmo), 2013; Deutsch, 1973). Accordingly, family conflict refers to *incompatibilities that can be expressed by people related through biological, legal, or equivalent ties.* As we discuss in later chapters, conflict issues and the precise manner in which family members communicate during conflict vary as a function of family members' relationships to each other, age, and other factors.

We should recognize that the reader likely has an implicit understanding of what everyday families look like. Koerner and Fitzpatrick (2006) presented a model of "family types" (similar to "marital types" discussed in chapter 2 and "stepfamily types" presented in chapter 3). According to Koerner and Fitzpatrick, two dimensions define families. The first is *conversational orientation,* or the extent to which families have open discussions about attitudes, feelings, values, and so forth. The second is *conformity orientation,* which concerns how family climates promote homogeneity in beliefs. By intersecting these two dimensions, one can derive four different types of families (Koerner & Fitzpatrick, 2006).

Families high in both conversational and conformity orientation are called *consensual.* Communication in these families reflects open discussion but, at the end of the day, consensus with the dominant belief system. So lively discussion is promoted so long as it coincides with what the parents think. *Pluralistic* families entertain high conversational orientations but low conformity. "Parents in these families are willing to accept their children's opinions and to let them participate in family decision making" (Koerner & Fitzpatrick, 2006, p. 169). Families that are low in conversation orientation but high on conformity orientation are called *protective*. In other words, parents expect obedience and do not care for much discussion. Finally, *laissez-faire* families involve low conversation orientation and low conformity orientation. Here families "let them be" (as the French implies). That is, family members interact infrequently and are "emotionally divorced from their families" (Koerner & Fitzpatrick, 2006, p. 169).

The effect of different family types in conflict communication is readily clear. Some families promote discussion of various issues and even welcome disagreement (pluralistic families), whereas other families welcome discussion but not disagreement (consensual families). And some families do not contain much communication among members and so do not provide a welcome context for disagreement. According to Koerner and Fitzpatrick (2006), consensual families express themselves emotionally (venting negative emotions) and seek social support from other members. Pluralistic family members also engage in solicitation of social support but they do not engage in much venting of negative emotion. Koerner and Fitzpatrick (2006, p. 170) explain that pluralistic family members avoid use of negative emotions precisely because they are not required to confine their discussions (i.e., conform). Next, protective families contain a combination of negative emotion and avoidance. The protective members do not have the communicative means to get their points across in a constructive manner, so they engage in these direct and indirect fighting tactics (Korner & Fizpatrick, 2006, p. 170). Finally, *laissez-faire* families contain infrequent, low intensity, and avoidant conflict communication. Because these family members are emotionally separated from each other, they have little interaction and, as a result, little conflict interaction.

Two important terms recur in the literature. These are *mediating* and *moderating effects*. A mediation effect occurs when one variable filters the effects of the independent variable on the dependent variable. For example, the level in trust of the parent can filter (mediate) the effects of parents' conflict on the child doing well in school. A moderating effect occurs when the effects of the independent variable change according to levels of the moderating factor. For example, high trust in the parent has no effect on the link between interparental conflict and school performance, whereas low trust in the parent has a negative effect on the relationship between interparental conflict and performance at school.

Theoretic Perspectives on Family Conflict

Theories are important because they explain people and processes. Theories also determine what should be studied (how you attempt to explain something leads to what should be explained) (Fisher, 1978). This section briefly offers three different theoretic approaches scholars have offered to study family conflict: systems, cognitive, and developmental. Although these three approaches do not represent all the perspectives one can take to examine family communication, one cannot delve into the topic of family conflict without running into the use of these theories. We present each as a conceptual context for understanding many of the findings in this book. The reader will recognize influences of these perspectives in definitions we reviewed above for both "family" and "conflict." Each major perspective contains an example theory that illustrates the broader perspective.

A Systems Perspective

One of the more integrating points of view on family communication behavior, including conflict, is systems theory. Systems theory offers a general approach regarding human behavior and provides an umbrella term for related approaches such as cybernetics and pragmatics, among others (see White & Klein, 2008, for a review). One theory that epitomizes the systems approach from a pragmatic perspective is Edna Rogers' relational communication theory (e.g., Millar & Rogers, 1976; Rogers, 2006).

Rogers' relational communication theory focuses on how interaction behavior defines the systems within families. Several properties of these systems should be mentioned. First, a family system is a whole; that is, the whole is greater than the sum of the parts. So the interactions between each family dyad require that one look at the message exchanges *between* them and not merely the behaviors or perceptions of one person.

Second, family members are *interdependent*. Interdependence means that one cannot be a family member without the other members present. The interdependence of all the members creates the family system. For example, Noller et al. (2000) found that conflict patterns between parents associated with the conflict behaviors that parents and children enacted. Likewise, parent–child interactions associated with sibling conflict behaviors.

Next, a *part/whole relationship* exists, such that each member and relationship is only part of the larger system. Here, "each level simultaneously influences and is influenced by the higher level. Thus each relational subsystem influences the larger family system and is influenced by the larger system" (Rogers, 2006, p. 118). Moreover, the part/whole relation implies that one subsystem has properties not present in other levels. For example, Ackerman et al. (2011) found that parents mutually influenced each other and siblings mutually influenced each other in terms of how positively they behaved during conflict interactions.

Fourth, the system is continually informing itself about its status through feedback. That is, systems are *self-regulating in order to maintain equilibrium*. There is a "cyclical flow" of information that provides feedback to its members. For instance, Robin and Foster's (1989) systems theory of adolescence describes how parents respond to adolescent changes in behavior that rock the family system, and how adolescents respond. The kernel idea here is that family members monitor information so as to maintain equilibrium.

Fifth, Rogers uses Bateson's (1951) concept of *two types of meanings – content and relational*. *Content messages* concern what is said, for example, "Give me the remote." *Relational messages* concern how something is said. For example, "Give me the remote" can be said as a request, as a command, as a tease, among other ways. "Content plays a part, but it is largely at the relational level that interactors indicate how they define their relationship" (Rogers, 2006, pp. 119–20).

Finally, family members can engage in *symmetrical and/or complementary communication*. Symmetrical refers to mirroring the other person's behavior, whereas complementary behavior refers to providing a message that endorses the other person's relational move. For example, if someone says "Come here," and a second person says "No, you come here," they have created a symmetrical interact (Millar & Rogers, 1976). However, if someone says "Come here," and the second person says "OK," they have created a complementary interact. As we shall see in chapter 2, these two forms of behavior can readily identify conflict message interacts. As Rogers (2006) stated, "Symmetry and complementarity exemplify the process of pattern identification and serve as prototypes for describing relational form" (p. 121).

Consider the following brief family conflict, which shows how family conflict is a system (from Vuchinich et al., 1988, p. 1296). The conflict begins when daughter (D) indicates she has plans to hang out with her friends, Sue and Rita. The mother (M) immediately objects and finds an ally in the father (F). The son (S) listens at first and then offers a possible solution.

Speaker	Message
D (to M):	Sue and Rita are coming over Saturday.
M (to D):	There you go again, looking for trouble.
	You know we're going to Grandma's Saturday.
D (to M):	You didn't say I had to go.
M (to D):	You know what I meant.
F (to D):	Don't argue with your mother. You're going.
D (to M):	But I've been planning this for weeks.
S (to F):	Why couldn't she have them over in the morning, then we could go to Grandma's in the afternoon?
D (to S):	You stay outta this. You're just makin' trouble.
S (to D):	I was trying to help, you jerk . . .
F:	I don't want to listen to this. You two button it.

[2.3 second silence]

M (to F):   Did Mr Baxter show you that big tomato?
F (to S):   Yeah, wasn't that something?

In terms of the part-whole feature of systems, note how the parents appear to adopt a coalition and the son wants to serve as a mediator of the entire discussion (turn 7). The example above also illustrates several subsystems through communication behavior: the daughter–mother relationship, the mother–father relationship, and the father–son relationship. However, to understand how each subsystem operates depends on the family as a whole and how equilibrium is kept to maintain the family. For example, the mother responds right away to her daughter with "There you go again, looking for trouble," and the daughter cautions her brother, "You stay outta this." However, the son replies with a symmetrical move, "I was trying to help, you jerk . . ." Once the parents regain equilibrium the mother changes the topic (after what appears to be two seconds of awkward silence).

A Cognitive Approach

Cognitive approaches tend to focus on meanings that people attach to conflict interactions. This view emphasizes how the mind works to process information related to conflict. For example, one study found that when people view their conflicts on videotape immediately after they occur, their recollections and interpretations of messages that occurred overlap with the other person's recollections and interpretations only by 3 percent at most (Sillars et al., 2000). Their recollections and inferences about conflicts are driven by *their own* experiences of the event (Sillars et al., 2000).

In brief, people's cognitive views of conflicts are limited, biased, and unreliable. Still, cognitions are all people have to make sense of conflict, and scholars have invested a great deal of time analyzing people's thoughts and feelings related to conflict communication. Grych and Fincham's (1990, 1993) cognitive-contextual model illustrates this approach.

Grych and Fincham's (1990) cognitive-contextual model concerns how interparental conflict affects children. This issue is

11

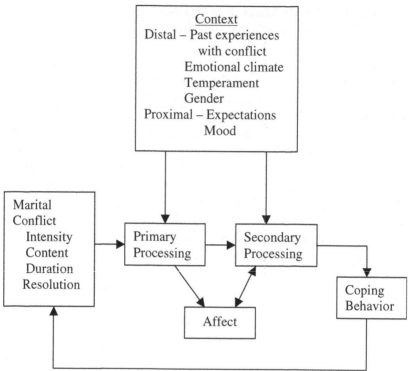

Figure 1.1   Grych and Fincham's Cognitive-Contextual Framework
Source: Grych & Fincham (1990, p. 278)

important, as interparental conflict management strongly affects children's psychological and social adjustment (see chapter 3). Several factors are presented. We discuss the primary and secondary processes only because these highlight the cognitive bases of the model. As Grych and Fincham stated, "Interparental conflict can be viewed as prompting three questions for children: 'What is happening?', 'Why is it happening?', 'What can I do about it?' Children's answers to these questions emerge from two proposed stages of processing, termed primary and secondary processing" (p. 281). Figure 1.1 presents their model.

Primary processing concerns appraisals that children make regarding how negative and relevant their parents' conflicts are.

The more intense and negative the conflicts, the more threatened the child will feel. Likewise, the more self-relevant the child perceives interparental conflict, the more threatened the child will feel. Such appraisals lead to negative emotions as well as secondary appraisals. As Grych and Fincham (1990) argued, "If conflict is not evaluated negatively or considered important, attention may shift away from the conflict and it may cease to affect the child. If the conflict is perceived as negative, significant, or self-relevant, further processing usually will occur" (p. 281). Thus, children attend to the extent to which their parents' conflict is negative, threatens them personally, and is related to them.

For example, Fosco and Grych (2010) examined how parents attempt to involve children in their conflicts, a phenomenon known as *triangulation*. As chapter 3 shows, children who are drawn into interparental conflicts find it difficult to cope with triangulation attempts. The researchers looked at the perceptions of interparental conflict and triangulation attempts among high-school students. Fosco and Grych found that the amount and severity of interparental conflict was associated with perceptions of triangulation and perceived threat, lack of coping, and self-blaming appraisals. Assessments of triangulation (feelings of being caught between parents) were then associated with self-blame. In brief, this study showed that perceptions of interparental conflict were more predictive than perceptions of triangulation in predicting how children made appraisals of interparental conflicts. These findings largely support the primary processing element of the cognitive-contextual model.

Secondary processing concerns attributions that children make regarding the cause(s) for the conflict and responsibility for the conflict. And this processing includes expectations that one has for managing one's responses to interparental conflict in a more or less successful manner. Several dimensions that compose attributional causes have been identified (Bradbury & Fincham, 1990). The most critical for conflict management are internality, stability, and globality. *Internality* refers to whether the cause is attributed to a feature of the other person (internal) or to an external force. *Stability* refers to whether the cause is seen as stable over time or temporary. *Globality* refers to whether the cause is seen as referring to a number of other events or isolated to the conflict issue. The most destructive attributions involve causes that are internal, stable, and global (Bradbury & Fincham, 1990). Grych and Fincham (1990) observed:

> This suggests that a child who views him or herself as the cause of parental conflict is likely to experience more distress than a child who attributes the cause of conflict to one or both parents or to outside circumstances. Similarly, a child who views conflict as caused by a stable and global factor (e.g., the parents do not love each other) is likely to be more upset by conflict than a child who makes an unstable, specific attribution (e.g., mother is in a bad mood), because it implies that the causes of the conflict are more likely to recur in the future and to affect many areas of family life. The expectation of future family turmoil or dissolution may lead to fear, sadness, or feelings of hopelessness in the child. (p. 282)

Next, expectations for dealing with interparental conflict concern the child's *self-efficacy* for conflict management, or the extent to which the child believes s/he has the wherewithal to manage turbulent situations. As might be anticipated, the higher the self-efficacy, the higher one's ability to manage conflict. Of course, this finding holds not only for children, but also for adults who decide on strategies for their own conflict interactions (e.g., Caughlin & Vangelisti, 2000). People with high self-efficacy (or high locus of control) for managing conflict are significantly more likely to engage in cooperative interaction tactics than are people who hold low self-efficacy (low locus of control) beliefs.

Finally, as Grych and Fincham's (1990, 1993) model shows, secondary processing affects the child's coping behavior (e.g., hiding in one's room vs. approaching a parent) which then might affect interparental conflict in the future. Also, several other factors affect the primary processes (e.g., contextual factors, emotions). However, the primary and secondary processes remain largely intact as key features of the model.

A Developmental Approach

Developmental approaches stress how children mature, and how communication behavior reflects different levels of maturation (as we emphasize in chapters 4 and 5). One of the clearest examples of a developmental approach is that of Robert Selman (1980, 2003). Key components to Selman's theory are perspective taking, perspective coordination, and interpersonal orientation. Each of these components is said to increase in sophistication as the child matures, from level 0 to level 4.

- **Level 0: Undifferentiated and egocentric.** Level 0 perspective taking occurs about the ages of 3–5, and this level of under-standing others is based entirely on understanding what self wants. Likewise, Level 0 perspective orientation entails a lack of understanding regarding how to coordinate interaction with other people. The child cannot see that they and other children and adults might interpret the same situation differently. Level 0 interpersonal orientation refers to how the child responds to the situation based on contextual information that the child has. However, the egocentric drive has the primary role when it comes to managing conflict with other children. That is, the child thinks largely in terms of self-interest that plays out rather compulsively (e.g., fight or flight behaviors).
- **Level 1: Differentiated and subjective perspective taking.** At this stage (ages 6–7), perspective taking involves understand-ing other children's points of view as distinct from one's own. That is, other people can see things differently. Level 1 perspective coordination entails differentiation of physical reality from psychological reality, which allows differentiation between intentional and unintentional actions. Level 1 orienta-tion coordination involves the exchange of compliance (e.g., "I will do this for you, if you do that for me").
- **Level 2: Self-reflective/second-person and reciprocal perspec-tive taking.** Level 2 social perspective taking occurs around the ages of 8–11. At this stage of development, people are now seen as complex in their thoughts and feelings, and one attempts to

assess the other person's view of self ("What do they think of my behavior?"). In Level 2 perspective coordination, the child can step outside of him/herself, self-reflect, and realize that other people can do the same. Here, reciprocity marks friendships and behaviors (friends at this stage, for example, will largely mirror each other's conflict behavior; Canary et al., 1995). Level 2 orientation coordination involves strategies to use psychological influence to change other people's minds and use self-persuasion to change one's own mind.

- **Level 3: Third-person and mutual perspective taking.** At this level (ages 10–15), social perspective taking involves stepping outside of oneself and recognizing that others are largely consistent. Mutual commitment to relationships as systems is the hallmark of this level of development. Level 3 perspective coordination involves seeing relationships as a system, a totality. Orientation coordination at this stage of development entails strategies that agree to or argue to let go of initial goals in order to achieve mutually acceptable goals.
- **Level 4: In-depth and societal-symbolic perspective taking.** At the highest level of development, which is said to occur in late adolescence and early adulthood (if at all), people's thoughts and actions can be viewed as inconsistent, which is part of human nature. Level 4 perspective coordination implies two features. First, because thoughts and actions are psychologically determined, they might not be perceived by either person. Second, people view each other's understandings of the other's view of their relationship based on meanings contained within verbal and nonverbal communication. Finally, Level 4 orientation coordination strategies would involve "Strategies that use both self and shared reflection to collaboratively transform (co-construct) both self's and other's goals in the creation of new projects with interdependent goals" (Selman, 2003, p. 38).

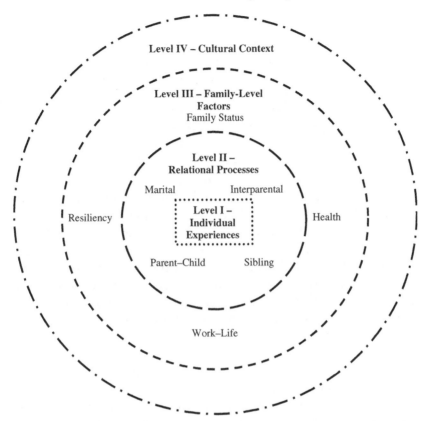

Figure 1.2 Multi-Level Model of Family Conflict

A Multilevel Model of Family Conflict

Figure 1.2 displays the model guiding this book. Four levels represent how family conflict reflects four levels. The broken lines represent that each level informs the other three. Similarly, the outer line is broken because all social systems are open rather than closed systems.

The most abstract level, Level IV, includes broad cultural factors that affect family conflict. Although it seems intuitive that such cultural dimensions as value orientations and expectations for family roles would constitute ongoing influences on family conflict interactions, research varies in terms of attention paid to these factors across different family subsystems. In general, not much research has focused on cultural effects and differences in family conflict processes (Bermúdez & Stinson, 2011; Feldman et al., 2010). To underscore the importance of culture in family conflict, we provide sections regarding culture in each of the chapters.

Level III concerns family-level factors. By *family-level factors* we mean influences that affect the entire family. These affect not only a subsystem of the family. Rather, they represent events that affect the entire family. *Family status* refers to the construction of the family – whether it be dual-parent homes (also called "married" or "intact" families), divorced homes, stepfamilies, or single-parent families, and so forth (for a review of family forms, see Socha & Yingling, 2010). *Health* concerns how one or more members of the family becomes physically or psychologically ill, and family members need to adjust to that event. *Work–life* concerns how family members balance their paid or unpaid work with living at home. As the research shows, these two domains of living intersect to affect conflict processes. Finally, *resiliency* (or family resilience) refers to unexpected events that present difficult challenges to family members. How family members respond to such events often entails conflict.

Level II concerns family conflict processes at the relational level. First, *marital* conflict involves disagreements and their management between people who are formally married. The lion's share of this research focuses on heterosexual partners in legally sanctioned unions. Next, *interparental conflict* refers to marital communication that has implications for the children. This body of research focuses on how marital conflicts affect children's welfare. *Parent–child* conflict includes conflict between parents and their offspring across the lifespan. Finally, *sibling* conflicts refer to how children from the same biological parents have their own set of problems between them that lead to conflict. Although we recognize the prevalence of stepfamilies that include half-siblings and step-siblings, the research focuses on siblings who share the same parents.

Finally, Level I concerns the individual's experiences regarding family conflict. This important level involves how people, especially children, make sense of family conflicts when they arise, progress, and end. In addition, Level I refers to a person's developmental stage, predispositions, and personalities (though the research on family conflict does not focus on personal tendencies or personality as much as it might; Ackerman et al., 2011). Level I also entails the effects of family conflict on the individual, including the individual's welfare (e.g., depression), physical health, and work–life management.

In light of our model of family conflict, we should state what this book emphasizes. First, as the chapter previews below show, in various ways we elaborate on the four levels of our multi-level model, either by devoting chapters to each topic (e.g., parent–child conflict) or by adding sections pertaining to some facet of the model (e.g., single-parent families). Second, we emphasize empirical studies to provide the best research we know on family conflict. By "empirical" we refer to both quantitative and interpretive qualitative investigations. The reader should keep in mind that our research base looks for general trends and associations – the findings do not necessarily depict your specific family or families. Finally, we attempt to provide a solid representation of this research. We cannot possibly provide an exhaustive review of each topic – the literature on family conflict is vast and complex, and the reader will get a sense of that. However, we can offer a fair representation of family conflict research that should be informative.

We have attempted to represent the best research on family conflict. This research led us to specific issues and findings. Importantly, the research provides background information about what needs to be understood about families and conflict, and it suggests how family members might engage in communication messages for managing conflict.

Chapter Previews

In chapter 2, we examine how conflict emerges and continues between the core members of the family – the marital partners.

The nature of marital communication, marital types, individual effects, and relational outcomes are discussed. In discussing individual effects, we focus on how conflict communication affects marital partners' depression and health. Finally, we examine the important conflict outcomes on marital quality (satisfaction) and divorce.

Next, chapter 3 discusses interparental conflict, divorce, and stepfamilies. The reader will see that interparental conflict affects other contexts (e.g., parenting closeness) as well as child adjustment. Spillover effects, feeling caught between parents, children's appraisals of interparental conflict, and relational implications between the parent and child are discussed. Research on how divorce affects the family is then discussed. We elaborate on how divorced couples manage conflict and how the children are involved. Finally, conflict in stepfamilies reveals the general emotional climate of the stepfamily as well as specific tactics that stepfamily members use. Approximately 65 percent of families are non-traditional, and most of these are stepfamilies. Not only do the children share zero genetic history with the stepfather or stepmother, they share zero history in terms of negotiating what it means to be a member of the family.

In chapter 4, we explore the research that emphasizes the child's development, beginning with a discussion of conflict between parents and their toddlers and preschoolers. Importantly, between the ages of two and four, children learn how to use communication strategically to get what they want. For the first time, perhaps, parents deal with the unexpected ways their babies assert themselves. The second age cohort concerns adolescence. This stage in children's lives includes many unexpected changes, including the ways hormonal changes and maturation affect conflicts teenagers have with their family members. We also review research about conflict between parents and their adult children, which remains an under-researched topic. Chapter 4 also presents findings regarding conflict between children and single parents. Given the burgeoning number of single parents, we believed that including this section was imperative.

Chapter 5 concerns sibling relationships, which are perhaps the longest-lasting relationships people have during their lifetimes. This chapter explains various facets of sibling conflict that provide readers a more complete and research-based understanding of sibling conflict. The chapter discusses sibling conflict interaction patterns in childhood and adolescence. The literature on adult siblings is sparse, and so it provides little information on the topic.

Chapter 6 discusses external matters that can affect family conflict processes. Families face a number of everyday and unexpected challenges at different points during the life cycle. Three bodies of research are discussed: work–life interface; health problems; and family resilience. First, a growing body of research investigates *work–life interface*, including family spillover effects and conflicts between demands of work and family. Second, a frequently researched challenge for families is health problems. Although short-term health problems undoubtedly influence family conflict, much research has focused on long-term health problems that become integrated into family life. Third, scholars have recently examined the concept of *family resilience*, that is, how families respond to unanticipated challenges, including unexpected economic hardship, health issues as described in the previous section, and death. This chapter focuses on the practical applications of using research findings to navigate family conflict in the face of negotiating work–life issues, chronic health problems, and resilience.

We hope the reader enjoys reviewing research and findings presented in each of the following chapters. More importantly, we hope this reading inspires further study and empirical investigations into family conflict communication.

2

Marital Conflict

Michael rises every day at 7:30 a.m., just in time to see his wife leaving for work. He is bothered by how sexy she looks. He thinks her outfit is not suitable for work. This topic has come up a few times before in their recent marriage.

    Michael: You aren't wearing that to work, are you?
    Brittany: Why not?
    Michael: Because it's tight and shows-off your curves.
    Brittany: Well, I have curves. So what? I wish you weren't so jealous.
    Michael: I'm not jealous. I just hate it when other men check you out.
    Brittany: Look, this is a conservative and professional outfit.
    Michael: I'd hate to see what a liberal outfit looks like!
    Brittany: You're just jealous and it's not attractive.
    Michael: I'm not jealous.
    Brittany: Look, I have to go.

As their wedding day approaches, engaged partners tend to have more and more conflicts (Braiker & Kelley, 1979). The reason for increased conflicts concerns how becoming interdependent with another person increases the "opportunities" for conflict (Braiker & Kelley, 1979). And conflicts likely increase after vows are exchanged (Kamp Dush & Taylor, 2012). Moreover, *how* partners manage them remains fairly stable over time (Van Doorn et al., 2007). Naturally, some people want to avoid conflict altogether, whereas other people thrive on it. Regardless, early married partners' opportunities for conflict are consequential. As this chapter shows, how marital partners manage conflict becomes critical to their well-being as individuals as well as to the well-being of their marriages and children. First, we discuss the nature of marital conflict.

The Nature of Marital Conflict

What is the nature of marital conflict? The answer to this question is impossible because marriage occurs in different forms with different rules and expectations. That is, marriage is not monolithic because it takes various forms (Fitzpatrick, 1988; Gottman, 1994; Kamp Dush & Taylor, 2012). A more realistic question would be *"What are the natures of marital conflict?"* In addition, couple conflict is fluid – what occurs in one episode of conflict connects to what happened before it and influences what occurs in later episodes. Moreover, couple conflict changes as partners age (with younger couples showing more confrontation; Kamp Dush & Taylor, 2012; Sillars & Wilmot, 1994). Finally, we should note that marital conflict has little structure, involves ambiguous objectives, and defies either partner's ability to recall what happened and what the partner said, even though both people might swear that they can recall everything accurately (Sillars & Weisberg, 1987; Sillars et al., 2000).

Topics regarding marital conflict vary (Kelley, 2012). The most important appear to be problems with communication, finances, division of chores, and showing affection (Gottman, 1994; Kelley, 2012). These topics represent important dimensions of marriage. For example, not being able to communicate with each other unravels the fabric of which the marriage is made. Likewise, conflicts regarding household division of labor can represent undue stress on the partner who does an unfair amount of work. However, any topic can become important, including how to spend leisure time, how to raise the children, in-laws, and even friends. Also, any topic can be a catalyst for marital conflict and seep into other areas of disagreement; all topics represent a chance to pick a fight.

Despite the above provisos, researchers have made some real progress in identifying the nature of marital conflict and its outcomes. We first discuss the "dual concerns approach" and different couple types for contextualizing marital conflict. Second, we present various communication strategies and tactics that marital researchers have uncovered. Next, we examine the effects of conflict on people's sense of well-being and health. Fourth, we explore the link between conflict management, relational satisfaction, and divorce. Finally, we conclude this chapter by looking at a few of the unexpected processes of marital conflict and how we might manage them.

Dual Concerns Approach of Marital Conflict

Decades of research have demonstrated the unequivocal importance that conflict communication has in discussions of relational stability and quality. Not that long ago, scholars often argued that interpersonal conflict presents the primary or only predictor of marital quality (e.g., Canary & Cupach, 1988). Recently, however, scholars have connected conflict processes with other relational processes (e.g., supportive messages; Sullivan et al., 2010). This connection of conflict to other processes to explain relational quality and stability has become known as the "dual concerns" approach.

For example, Caughlin and Huston (2006) found that two factors predict divorce: affection and antagonism. They found that high levels of affection are needed at the outset of marriage as well as over the course of marriage. Not surprisingly, high levels of antagonism and low levels of affection lead to divorce right away (i.e., within two years). As their data show, low levels of affection also predicted divorce between 7 and 14 years, even though antagonism was only moderate. These findings coincide with research by Gottman and Levenson (2002) who found that negative conflict primarily predicted divorce the first seven years of marriage but lack of affection predicted divorce after 7 years.

Figure 2.1 presents a dual concerns model by Canary and Lakey (with Marmo) (2013). This model emphasizes how cooperative and competitive conflict tactics work in conjunction with positive

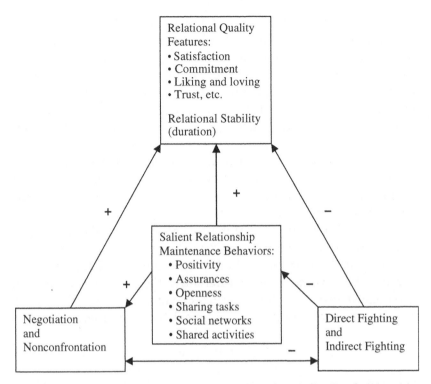

Figure 2.1   Links among Cooperative and Competitive Conflict, Relationship Maintenance Behaviors, Stability, and Relational Quality Features

Note: A positive sign indicates a positive association between factors; a negative sign indicates an inverse association between factors.
Source: Canary and Lakey (with Marmo), 2013.

and proactive relational maintenance strategies to affect marital quality. Relational maintenance strategies represent communicative processes that married people use in an ongoing and frequent way to keep their relationships as they want them (Canary et al., 2002; Stafford & Canary, 2006).

Commonly used maintenance strategies include *positivity* (being upbeat), *openness* (discussing the relationship), *assurances* (stressing one's commitment), *sharing tasks* (e.g., household chores), *social networks* (e.g., relying on friends and family to support the marriage), and *shared activities* (e.g., doing leisure activities together) (Canary & Lakey (with Marmo), 2013; Stafford & Canary, 2006). In this light, conflict occurs in the overall context of how well partners engage in positive and proactive strategies to maintain their marriages. Both conflict and maintenance communication should be acknowledged when discussing whether marriages succeed or fail. For instance, Kamp Dush and Taylor (2012) summarized their findings accordingly: "A stronger belief in lifelong marriage, shared decision making, and husbands sharing a greater proportion of housework were associated with an increased likelihood of membership in a high happiness, low conflict marriage, and a decreased likelihood of a low marital happiness group" (p. 341).

Note how in figure 2.1 that maintenance and conflict behaviors interact to affect relational quality. The point is that other positive relational processes combine with conflict to affect relational quality and divorce. Stated differently, the way conflict affects marriage depends on how partners manage conflict as well as provide an overall positive environment for each other.

Marital Types

Different types of marriages exist and couples differ quite a bit in what they consider competent conflict behaviors. More precisely, Fitzpatrick (1988) discovered three "pure" types of marriages. First, partners in a Traditional marriage endorse traditional values, have high interdependence, and engage in conflicts only to the extent they are important (vs. simply bothersome). Independent partners do not hold traditional values, are moderately interdependent, and confront each other rather routinely. Separate marriages contain a traditional ideology, little interdependence, and infrequent conflict. Using observational data of marital conflicts alone, Gottman (1994) found evidence for these pure couple types and their behaviors. Finally, apart from these pure types, Fitzpatrick found a sizable minority of people who have "mixed" marriages. Here, one person adopts one form of marriage schemata and the partner adopts a different form. The most common mixed couple is the traditional wife and separate husband.

Kelley (2012, pp. 106–7) discusses differences in conflict due to couple type. Traditional partners engage in conflict over important issues, are conciliatory, and focus on the content of conflicts more so than the relational implications of conflicts. Independent partners readily engage in conflicts, are highly expressive (both delivering and seeking expression), and use negotiation to get their way. In an opposite manner, separate partners avoid conflict, have difficulty overcoming their emotional distance with each other, and suppress open discussion. As this summary suggests, what constitutes satisfactory conflict communication differs quite substantially based on couple type.

Being in a Mixed marriage can be quite frustrating, because each partner has different mental models for how one should behave in marriage and manage conflict. Remember that the most common mixed marriage involves a Traditional wife and a Separate husband. Consider the following example, which reflects a Traditional/Separate mixed marriage. Here, the wife ("F") wants increased interaction with her husband ("M"); he wants more autonomy to "play" with his friends. Here, the simple issue of how to spend leisure time reflects a larger underlying issue of how they define their marriage. Note as well how he closes off the conflict rather abruptly – a common tactic for Separates.

Speaker	Message
M:	I never get enough time with my friends.
	Janet doesn't really have many *close* friends that she spends a lot of time with like I do. But . . .
F:	But the problem is, some of *his* friends are just him and his friends.
	Why can't it be him and his friends and me?
M:	Because it's just two people,
	it's just *guys* hanging out.
	We don't want girls.
F:	I let you hang out with your guy friends, usually.
M:	You're doing better.
F:	You play a lot of sports.
	If you didn't play so many sports then I would let you hang out with more of your friends more.

M: Then I wouldn't be in shape.
F: Yes you would.
M: No I wouldn't.
F: Yes you would.
M: I let you do anything with your friends, always.
        I never tell you no.
F: That's because I don't go and *play* with my friends as much as you want me to.
M: But you're not as close with friends. So you want to be –
F: No, because you're *my* best friend and I'd rather be with *you*.
M: Okay, alright next question. ....

The point to this discussion on marital types concerns how people's satisfaction depends on the blueprint for marriage they have. How Traditionals communicate during conflict differs from Independents, who differ from Separates, who differ from Traditionals. And partners in these marriages are largely satisfied. Having a mixed couple type, however, appears to be less functional and can lead to dissatisfying conflict management messages. Many people enter marriage believing that they and their partner share in their blueprints for marriage. Not until they try to build their marriage do they realize that they have very different plans.

Marital Conflict Strategies and Tactics

Throughout this book, we refer to communication behavior processes. Much of the research we cite concerns communication strategies and tactics, although studies also assess conflict frequency or intensity. These strategies and tactics are often observed by trained coders or self-reported by participants. *Strategies* refer to the general approach that people take, whereas *tactics* make the strategies happen in real time. In other words, strategies represent the general choices people make about what to do and tactics institute those strategies in real time.

To give the reader a glimpse of the conflict communication

behaviors in marriage, we present one way of categorizing conflict communication behavior. Van de Vliert and Euwema (1994) analyzed conflict strategies and tactics. Their comprehensive review yielded four different general approaches for managing conflict: *negotiation tactics*, which are direct and cooperative; *direct fighting tactics*, which are direct and competitive; *nonconfrontation*, which are indirect and cooperative; and *indirect fighting*, which are indirect but competitive (often called "withdrawal"). Sillars et al. (2004) could readily categorize various conflict behaviors found in marital interaction coding systems into four quadrants: Direct and Cooperative (negotiation); Direct and Competitive (direct fighting); Indirect and Cooperative (nonconfrontation); and Indirect and Competitive (indirect fighting). Recently, Sillars and Canary (2013) refined these categories into smaller but representative conflict strategies and tactics. Now, we have further synthesized the Sillars and Canary effort. Table 2.1 reports our categorization of conflict codes (based on Sillars and Canary, 2013).

The reader should note how each marital conflict strategy can

Table 2.1 Communication Strategies and Tactics

Negotiation (Direct and Cooperative):
Accepts responsibility: Suggests that "I" or "we" are responsible for the problem.
Approves: Acknowledges and approves of the partner's actions, statements, or explanations.
Describes issues: Defines or describes the conflict issue, without blame.
Seeks disclosure: Asks the partner for his/her ideas and feelings, including criticism.
Problem solves: Suggests course of action, and/or accepting the other person's course of action.
Makes conciliations: Supports the other; accepts responsibility.
Mind-reads (positive): Attributes the partner's behavior to positive thoughts or motives.
Compromises: Attempts to split the difference on an area of disagreement.
Proposes change: Proposes a termination or decrease in behavior or an increase in behavior.
Reconciles: Shows concern for the partner's feelings, attempts to make-up, offers help or reassurance.

Table 2.1 *(continued)*

Direct Fighting (Direct and Competitive):
Blames other: Criticizes other, refuses or avoids responsibility.
Uses personal attacks: Puts down other, uses sarcasm, ridicules, and so forth.
Threatens other: Indicates some harm will come if partner does not comply.
Coerces: Uses external power (e.g., finances), commands the person to do something, induces guilt.
Confronts: Rejects the other person's statements, calls the other person's bluffs, makes hostile imperatives, asks hostile questions.
Mind-reads (negative): States that negative attitudes or motives underlie partner's behaviors, said with negative emotion.
Interrupts: Disallows partner to complete thought in a competitive manner.

Nonconfrontation (Indirect and Cooperative):
Changes topic: Moves the discussion from the current topic to a different one.
Denies: Denies that a problem exists (said with neutral affect), evades presence of conflict.
Disengages: Expresses desire not to discuss an issue.

Indirect Fighting (Indirect and Competitive):
Manages topic: Terminates discussion before it has reached completion and limits discussion.
Conveys negative emotion: Communicates contempt, disgust, whining, sadness, depression, and other negative states.
Withdraws: Gives-up on the conversation, stonewalls, gives silent treatment, leaves the scene.
Uses negative humor: Attempts to intimidate through use of humor.

be represented by a variety of tactics. Accordingly, when marital researchers speak of "constructive" or "positive" conflict (i.e., negotiation), several alternative tactics can institute this direct and cooperative approach. For example, one can be direct and cooperative by problem solving, offering disclosure, seeking reconciliation, and so forth. "Destructive" or "negative" tactics are direct and competitive, including negative mind-reading, hostile imperatives, denial of responsibility, etc. The critical issue in the conflict literature is not whether all tactics are included in the research; rather, the issue is whether the various marital strategies are adequately represented.

In a separate line of inquiry, Edna Rogers has created a coding scheme to identify whether relational control moves represent dominance, equivalence/transitory, and submissive behaviors (Rogers & Farace, 1975). We offer a brief summary with examples from her manual. Dominance is represented with a "one-up" arrow (↑); equivalence is noted with a "one-across" arrow (→); and submissiveness is depicted with a "one-down" arrow (↓). Consider the following example and note how one can see how the system requires both people and their message behaviors over time to understand the system relationship. The issue concerns her wanting him to go to Bible study on Thursday nights.

Speaker	Message	
M:	Thursday night now.	
	Monday, Tuesday, Wednesday, Friday,	
	Saturday, now Thursday too?	→
F:	Now it's *Thursday* night bible study.	↑
M:	I have too many other things going on.	
	It's like I need to kill another night.	↑
F:	What do you have going on besides working and	
	watching sports on TV?	↑
M:	I just like to have *some* free time.	→
F:	That *is* free time.	→
	That is a *fun* thing to do.	→
M:	For *you*.	↑
F:	No, for *you*.	↑
M:	Oh so *that's* the deal?	↑
	That's why you are not cooking?	
	Because I don't go to Thursday night bible study?	
F:	No, I'm just making you a deal that I'll do that.	
	I'm not cooking because I'm a full-time worker	
	at a job just like you are.	
	From seven to five I work.	↑

Note how this married couple engages in a lot of competition. These are symmetrical dominance behaviors, also known as *competitive symmetry*, where the husband and wife mirror each other's attempts to control the conversation. Backing down from continued rigidity of competitive symmetry is functional, whereas continued competitive symmetry represents a dissatisfying and dysfunctional system (Courtright et al., 1979; Rogers, 2006). Submissive symmetry would also tend to be dysfunctional (e.g., "What do you want to do tonight?" "I don't care – whatever you want is fine with me." "Well, it's your turn. What do you want?" "Whatever you want is what I want.")

Individual Outcomes of Marital Conflict

Readers who have been in serious, committed romantic relationships can attest to the potentially devastating impacts that conflict can have. A salient factor when discussing such impacts concerns the role of depression. In a word, depression can affect how people manage conflict and how people manage conflict can affect their depression. In addition, research has documented how marital conflict can affect the individual's health. Recently, Canary and Lakey (with Marmo) (2013) reviewed this literature. We rely on their review for the following material, adding other research.

The Depression-Conflict Link

In general, depressed people tend to have poor social skills, rely more on confronting and negative tactics, engage in demand-withdraw patterns, and rely less on cooperative and direct communication during conflict (Henne et al., 2007; Segrin 2000). Moreover, these behaviors are "corroborated by their spouses, when engaged in marital interaction" (Segrin, 2000, p. 385). For example, Du Rocher Schudlich et al. (2004) found that experiences of depression led to both partners' use of angry and depressing messages. The conflict tactics that were used in reaction to depression included verbal hostility, defensiveness, withdrawal, insults, and nonverbal displays of anger and sadness. As this study suggests, both the depressed person and the partner engage in negative conflict tactics. Other research has shown that demanding, withdrawing, and avoiding behaviors tend to increase depression in one person and anger with the other (e.g., Henne et al., 2007). Most of us want to believe that we are cared for, that we are valuable and valued, and that life is fundamentally good. Siffert and Schwarz (2011) examined how conflict affected participants' subjective well-being. Subjective well-being was operationally defined as a *lack* of depression, self-esteem, and life satisfaction. These authors found that four conflict tactics negatively affected marital partners' subjective well-being: "It happens that I throw insults on her/him," "I explode and get out of control," "I launch personal attacks," and "I say things that aren't meant." Also, withdrawal had negative but less severe effects on the partner's subjective well-being.

As mentioned, depression leads to negative conflict communication which, in turn, increases one's depression. As Choi and Marks (2008) found, "Depressive symptoms led to more marital conflict, which, in turn, led to more depressive symptoms over time" (p. 384). Du Rocher Schudlich et al. (2011) found that angry, depressive, and constructive conflict communication behaviors filtered how marital satisfaction affected one's depression. That is, the communication of anger and depression increased partner depression regardless of marital satisfaction levels. This finding supports a cyclical view of the conflict-depression link and suggests that constructive conflict can help interrupt the conflict-depression cycle. Whitton et al. (2007) found that destructive conflict affected women's depression a year later. However, these effects were reduced when the women believed that their relationships would continue.

One reason for the conflict-depression cycle resides in perceptions of the other marital partner. Do people perceive greater similarity of negative conflict messages when depressed? If they do perceive similarity in behavior then the two partners would likely engage in a self-fulfilling prophecy and increase the use of those behaviors. Papp et al. (2010) examined whether depressed versus non-depressed partners perceived their conflict behaviors similarly. They found that when the husband or wife was depressed then the wife perceived that what she did during conflict matched what she thought her husband did. More precisely, wives perceived that they and their husbands behaved in similar ways in expressing anger, sadness, and fear. "That is, in the context of higher spousal depression, the emotional transmission of wives' negative emotions in marital conflict was stronger than in lower spousal depression" (p. 383). One reason why wife emotional transmission occurred (vs. husband) is that women tend to mind relationship issues more and so attend to the occurrence of these negative emotions, and in doing so make mistakes as to the similarity of their partner's conflict behaviors. Interestingly, however, regardless of depression levels or sex, both people tended to believe that their partners behaved similarly in their expression of anger (p. 377).

Segrin's (2000) *social skills deficit vulnerability model* is helpful in understanding the depression-conflict link. "It is, therefore, the combination of poor social skills and negative life events that are thought to produce depressive distress. The reasoning behind this model is that people with good social skills can marshal the kind and quantity of social support that will be effective for coping with the stressful events. On the other hand, people with poor social skills are expected to (a) experience more stressors, and (b) be less able to secure assistance and social support for dealing with those stressors when they do occur" (pp. 394–5). Conflict is a stressor. Accordingly, depressed people experience more conflict stress but cannot "secure assistance and social support" from their partners when dealing with conflict. The outcome of these negative experiences for the depressed person and their partners is continued negative conflict and depression.

Even when people want to help their depressed partners, they feel caught in a double-bind. According to inconsistent nurturing control theory (Duggan & Le Poire, 2006), people want to nurture their partners in order to reduce their depression but also desire to have their partner remain dependent on him/her. Depressed people receive rewards from partner nurturance but also want to experience more happiness (Duggan, 2007). Given these inconsistent goals, it is difficult to know how to respond to a partner who is depressed (or if oneself is depressed). Hence, people likely attempt to show cooperation but then revert to competition now and then in the context of depressing conflicts.

The research literature shows precisely how and why people perpetuate depression through conflict. This research also emphasizes how depression is as much a communicative phenomenon as it is an individual experience. In other words, one should not engage in communication tactics of anger, demand, sadness, avoidance, or withdrawal during conflict interactions. Such behaviors simply lead to and perpetuate depressive symptoms and reduce one's sense of well-being. Such behaviors should be avoided, even if these negative and avoidant conflict tactics are used only inconsistently. Rather, the *consistent* use of negotiation conflict tactics (table 2.1) appears most helpful.

Individual Health

As indicated above, how people manage conflict directly affects their physical health. Researchers have specifically identified three areas where conflict affects one's health: the cardiovascular system, the hormonal system, and the immunological system.

The cardiovascular system
How individuals engage in marital conflict influences heart disease (Suarez, 2004). For example, hostility and anger affect the fatality of coronary artery disease (CAD). Boyle et al. (2004) followed patients with CAD for approximately 15 years. They found that CAD participants who responded to others with hostility (e.g., showing aggressiveness) were much more likely to die than CAD participants who did not respond with hostile tactics. Additionally, Bliel et al. (2004) found that the tendency to react in anger and hostility increased people's levels of carotid artery atherosclerosis (lesions in arteries leading to the brain), a leading cause of stroke, heart attacks, and other heart diseases. Finally, Miller et al. (1999) found that typically hostile husband use of anger was associated with higher levels of blood pressure, cortisol, and other negative bio-markers.

The endocrine system

The endocrine system refers to how glands generate chemicals that tell other organs to perform in particular ways. Research by Kiecolt-Glaser and colleagues (e.g., Kiecolt-Glaser et al., 1993) has shown that conflict communication markedly affects hormones that regulate reactions to stress and metabolism. Kiecolt-Glaser et al. (1993) found that increases in epinephrine (also known as adrenaline) and norepinephrine occurred in even healthy and happy newlyweds. The key to the increases in hormones was whether they used negative problem-solving communication. Epinephrine and norepinephrine are largely responsible for increases in heart rate, blood pressure, etc. Also, Kiecolt-Glaser et al. (1993) found that negative conflict interaction affected other hormones, reducing one's health. In a similar manner, Suarez et al. (1998) found that hostile people had significantly higher norepinephrine, cortisol, and testosterone scores. Prolonged changes in hormones, such as the ones mentioned above, through the consistent use of negative conflict tactics likely entail debilitating health effects, such as hypertension, heart disease, and obesity, which in turn negatively affect one's quality of life and lead eventually to death. Chronic increases of stress hormones due to poor conflict management increase cardiovascular reactivity (CVR) (Loving et al., 2004). However, cooperative conflict tactics do not affect one's health in negative ways.

The immunological system

Competitive conflict also taxes one's immune system. "Immune dysregulation may be one core mechanism for a spectrum of conditions associated with aging, including cardiovascular disease, osteoporosis, arthritis, Type 2 diabetes, certain cancers, and frailty and functional decline," as well as wound healing (Kiecolt-Glaser et al., 2002, p. 537). Kiecolt-Glaser et al. (2002) found that even healthy couples suffer from decreases in immune functioning if they engage in negative conflict tactics.

Conflict also affects the immune system's response to the common cold. In one study, conflict was linked to whether people catch a cold once they are infected with a cold virus. In a study by

Cohen et al. (1998), participants reported on various events that increased their levels of stress at one month, three months, and six months. Cohen et al. then squirted one of two cold viruses into the noses of the volunteers. Participants who reported stress for more than one month were significantly more likely to catch a cold than participants with low stress. More exactly, participants who endured ongoing interpersonal conflicts were approximately three times more likely to catch a cold than were those without ongoing conflict. Cohen et al. concluded that "Chronic stressors based on interpersonal conflicts . . . and problems associated with work [e.g., unemployment] were primarily responsible for the associations found in this study" (1998, p. 221).

The use of negative conflict tactics represents continued negative stressors that harm the body and accelerate death (Umberson et al., 2006). And such tactics can affect one's health indirectly as well, for example, by increasing one's depression that then leads to health risks (Kiecolt-Glaser et al., 2010). Over time, continued episodes of competitive, negative conflict would harm the communicator in dramatic and negative ways. As Choi and Marks (2008) indicated, "When marital conflict undermines physical health, it has multiple ramifications over time in terms of additional further declines in mental and physical health" (p. 388). In short, the reader will likely live better and longer if you react to family problems with calm and cooperative conflict messages.

Relational Outcomes of Marital Conflict

Marital Quality

How conflict affects marriage garnered the interest of social psychologists, communication scholars, and others primarily from the 1970s through the 1990s. In the 1970s, scholars discovered the powerful role that conflict communication plays in affecting and reflecting marital quality (satisfaction) (Raush et al., 1974). By the 1990s, full-blown theories had emerged that connected conflict communication to marriage, the most notable being Gottman's in 1994.

Here is a brief representative summary of findings regarding how conflict communication connects to marital satisfaction (e.g., Birditt et al., 2010; Canary et al., 1995; Gottman, 1994): (1) negative conflict strategies and tactics more than positive messages associate with marital satisfaction; (2) reciprocation of negative emotions is especially damaging; (3) unhappy couples engage in increased amounts of negative conflict communication over the span of a conversation; (4) direct and cooperative messages are most functional most of the time; (5) nonverbal behaviors, such as showing contempt, can powerfully affect satisfaction; (6) nonverbal behaviors, such as talking rapidly and loudly, can also combine with verbal behaviors to affect satisfaction; (7) sequences of conflict tactics, such as the demand–withdraw pattern, can predict whether couples are satisfied; (8) some sequences – such as exchanges of meta-communication – can be functional or not depending on whether the nonverbal emotions accompanying them are positive or negative; (9) ongoing withdrawal reflects a dysfunctional marriage; and (10) the conflict-satisfaction link is affected by marital type (as discussed earlier in this chapter).

As indicated in point 1 above, negative conflict tactics reduce marital quality. For example, Noller et al. (1994) assessed couples' communication and relationship satisfaction just prior to marriage and then during the first two years of marriage. They found that married partners did not vary that much in their conflict tactics over time. Rather, partners tended to use the same conflict tactics over the two years they were observed. As expected, satisfied partners engaged in less negativity. Such negative behaviors they did *not* use included the Direct Fighting tactics of threats, coercion, and so forth. More satisfied partners were also less likely to avoid or withdraw from conflict compared to partners with lower satisfaction scores. Likewise, Birditt et al. (2010) found that the use of destructive tactics and exchanges involving withdrawal led to divorce, whereas constructive tactics reduced the likelihood of divorce over a 16-year period.

As mentioned in point 7 above, conflict sequences predict relational satisfaction. That is, conflict tactics emerge in real time in sequences of behavior. Table 2.2 lists representative negative con-

Table 2.2   Examples of Negative Reciprocation Patterns

1. **Demand–withdraw:** One person attempts to discuss an issue, often negatively; the other person refuses or otherwise denies the problem or deflects the issue
2. **Complaint–countercomplaint:** A complaint by one person is followed by a counter-complaint by the other (Gottman, 1982)
3. **Proposal–counterproposal:** A proposal by one partner is met immediately by a proposal by the other partner (Gottman, 1982)
4. **Disagreement–disagreement:** Disagreement is reciprocated and/ or develops refutations against another person's points (Canary et al., 1991)
5. **Defensiveness–defensiveness (indifference):** Behaviors that are threatening or punishing to others and reciprocally invite and produce defensive behaviors in return (Alexander, 1973)
6. **Attack–counterattack:** One person's criticism, showing contempt and so forth are countered by the second person doing the same
7. **Metacommunication–metacommunication (w/negative feelings):** Statements about the process of communication are continuous (Gottman, 1982)
8. **Mind-reading (negative affect):** Making attributions of emotions, opinions, states of mind, etc., to a spouse, delivered with negative affect; it is responded to as if it were a criticism; it is disagreed with and elaborated upon, usually with negative affect (Gottman, 1982)
9. **Summarizing self:** A statement by one spouse, followed by a statement from the other spouse that evaluates the speaker's previous statements (Gottman, 1979)
10. **Complain–justification:** Individual-oriented blaming that discloses discontentment and resentment indirectly, followed by the other's individual-oriented act which persists in clarifying one's own position regardless of other's feelings/idea (Ting-Toomey, 1983)

Note: From Cupach et al. (2010) with the assistance of Melissa Marks; published in Canary & Lakey (with Marmo) (2013).

flict sequences and table 2.3 presents positive sequences (Canary & Lakey (with Marmo), 2013; Cupach et al., 2010). Some negative sequences include agreement–disagreement, proposal–counterproposal, attack–defend, and demand–withdraw (table 2.2). More positive sequences include validation, contracting, and supportiveness–supportiveness (table 2.3).

Table 2.3 Examples of Positive Reciprocation Patterns

1. **Validation (argument exchange):** Comment followed by the other with "assent codes" (Gottman, 1982)
2. **Contracting:** Direct modification of one's own point of view (Gottman, 1982)
3. **Convergence:** Understanding and/or agreement with one anothers' arguables, the convergence is either explained and/or leads to new ideas (Canary et al., 1991)
4. **Supportiveness–supportiveness:** Genuine information seeking and information giving are reciprocated (Alexander, 1973)
5. **Cajoling (coaxing–coaxing):** Mutual-oriented act that attempts to make the partner feel good about himself/herself before making explicit any other motivation behind the act (e.g., flattering other, gentle appealing, jokes) (Ting-Toomey, 1983)
6. **Metacommunication-metacommunication (w/positive feelings):** Brief statements about the constructive process of communication (Gottman, 1979).
7. **Socioemotional (description–question):** Descriptive statements concerning one's feelings, followed by statements that ask about the partner's emotion (Ting-Toomey, 1983)
8. **Task-oriented (question–question):** Statements that ask for factual information or request further elaboration of task-oriented points, followed by asking for information or further elaboration from the other spouse criterion (Ting-Toomey, 1983)
9. **Task-oriented (question–description):** Statements that ask for factual information or request further elaboration of task-oriented points, followed by issue-oriented factual statements concerning the past, present, or future (Ting-Toomey, 1983)
10. **Mind-reading (neutral, positive affect):** Making attributions of emotions, opinions, states of mind, etc., to a spouse with neutral or positive affect, it is then responded to as if it were a question about feelings; it is agreed with and elaborated (Gottman, 1982)
11. **Summarizing (spouse or both):** Any statement by the other speaker that summarizes the previous statements of the other person (Gottman, 1979)

Note: From Cupach et al. (2010) with the assistance of Melissa Marks; published in Canary & Lakey (with Marmo) (2013).

The sequence that has received the lion's share of research is the demand–withdrawal pattern (Caughlin & Vangelisti, 2006). In this pattern, one person attempts to approach the partner about some issue, perhaps even through nagging and complaining, and that partner denies there is a problem, through avoidance, denial of any problem, refusal to discuss it, and so forth (Caughlin & Vangelisti, 2006; Christensen & Heavy, 1990). The demand–withdrawal pattern has been found to be detrimental to marital satisfaction. As one can imagine, this pattern is very frustrating and reflects deeper problems in the marriage (including unresolved conflicts).

The following sequence illustrates how specific tactics are used to construct a demand–withdraw pattern (from Canary & Lakey (with Marmo), 2013, pp. 30–1). The wife ("F") proposes a negotiation (that he listen to her idea) (see table 2.1). Instead of listening to her, the husband ("M") argues that she should cook as if she had kids to feed. This message is clearly Direct Fighting. In turn 9, the wife responds with a *hostile question* that is followed by a *rejection* of the husband's argument (we have one child, and he is an adult).

Speaker	Message
F:	Cooking meals, let's just start with cooking meals.
	Okay I'll make you a deal. I'll make you a deal on cooking meals.
M:	[loudly] NO! I AM <u>NOT GOING TO STOP WATCHING</u> (brief pause, softer) baseball games just because. . .
F:	[interrupting] No, I wasn't go to say that.
	I wasn't going to say that.
M:	It's not like. . . Okay. . .
F:	I mean, do you want to <u>solve</u> the cooking meal problem or do we just want to fight about it?
M:	No because. . .
F:	[interrupting] Would you like me to make the meals?
	Then I want something back,
	that's all.
	I'll make you a deal.

M: No!
            I think you just do it,
            because it's your responsibility if you had, you know,
            kids to feed and stuff.
F: Why do you say that kids to feed thing?
            We have one kid;
            he's a grown-up.
            He can cook for himself.

In contrast, the following interaction shows how both marital partners engage in *validation* sequences. One can also hear a difference in emotional tone between the above example and the following one. After the discovery that they have a conflict, the wife engages in validation before she states the rationale for her disagreement. The husband concedes and then validates in the final statement.

Speaker	*Message*
M:	I looked at your outline when you were out of the room.
	Can I make a suggestion on how you frame your idea?
F:	Well . . . no.
M:	(ignoring her): It concerns the first sentence.
F:	I wrote that a long time ago.
M:	OK, but do you mind?
F:	I appreciate your feedback, more than you know.
	And I enjoy sharing my ideas with you at night.
	But I want to set the rules on this:
	Your helping me simply isn't right.
	I need to do my own work.
	I will show you my papers once they are submitted.
M:	OK. (pause) That was great – I really like how you said that.

In addition, research shows that the expression of emotion during conflict varies according to how fairly each partner feels. Equity theory holds that each partner should receive the same amount of outcomes divided by inputs as his or her partner (Hatfield et al., 1985). So fairness is determined not only by what each person gets out of the relationship, but also by what each person puts into the relationship (Sprecher, 2001). So partners might get the same amount of rewards, but if one works harder than the other then this relationship is unfair. People who feel fairly treated are much more satisfied than people who feel they are being taken advantage of (Van Yperen & Buunk, 1990) and much more likely to use positive and proactive maintenance strategies (Stafford & Canary, 2006). As one might anticipate, people who feel taken advantage of are more likely to express anger than people who feel equitably treated (Guerrero et al., 2008). Accordingly, equity affects partner's emotional reactions to each other as well as satisfaction with the partner.

Divorce

Despite the best intentions on their wedding day, many marriages dissolve. Perhaps the leading expert on how conflict affects divorce is Gottman. This section briefly summarizes Gottman's (1994) model of divorce that focuses on how conflict is communicated and processed (though keep in mind that conflict combines with positive relational processes in predicting divorce).

Figure 2.2 presents Gottman's model of divorce. As the reader can see, the model begins with conflict tactics (upper left corner). In particular, four conflict tactics are especially "corrosive." Indeed, Gottman labels these the "Four Horsemen of the Apocalypse" to indicate how terrible these behaviors are to marital stability. And these behaviors are said to occur in this disintegrating sequence: (1) *complain/criticize* concerns registering what you do not like about the partner; (2) *contempt* concerns one's disdain for the partner, largely communicated nonverbally (e.g., nose shrug); (3) *defensiveness* reveals one's ongoing negative sensitivity to the partner; and (4) *stonewalling* concerns refusal to discuss relational issues. If marital partners combine positive, constructive conflict behaviors with negative, destructive behaviors at a 1:1 ratio, then the marriage is "balanced" for instability. If marital partners combine positive, constructive conflict behaviors with negative behaviors at a 5:1 ratio, then the marriage is "balanced" for stability.

Second, in the upper right corner, we see that people perceive

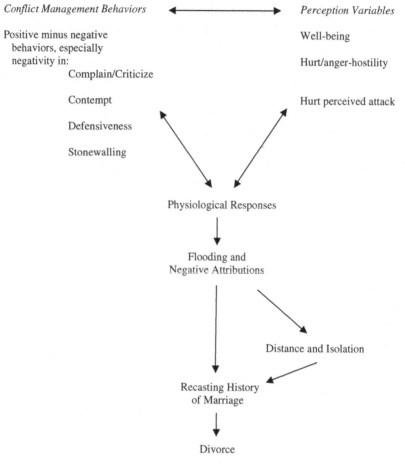

Figure 2.2 Gottman's Model of Divorce
Adapted from Gottman (1994), p. 370.

these conflict behaviors. Two general reactions occur. First, if the partner uses a 5:1 ratio of positive/negative conflict tactics, then one feels a sense of well-being. Next, if the partner uses a 1:1 ratio of positive/negative conflict tactics, then one feels hurt and anger/hostility or hurt with perceived attack, or both.

Third, people experience physiological arousal based on the communicative tactics and their immediate reactions to those behaviors. As the preceding section on health suggests, one's cardiovascular reactivity (CVR) would likely increase as the result of negative conflict in particular. Such increases in one's CVR and other physiological responses (e.g., sweating) would likely lead to the next part of the model.

Fourth, two important processes occur. The first is *flooding*, or the experience of not being able to process and make sense of one's physiological reactions. Here one is "surprised, overwhelmed, and disorganized by your partner's expression of negative emotions" (p. 21). The second important process involves making negative attributions about the conflict event and partner. In brief, *attributions* are explanations that people give about people's behavior, events, and attitudes. Making negative explanations about the partner (e.g., he is a liar) constitutes "the initial catastrophic change" in the marriage. In other words, once you attribute the cause of conflict problems and communication to a persistent problem residing in the partner (which can also explain other behaviors besides conflict) then the marriage is doomed. The use of negative attributions is so critically important that Zillman (1993) advised the following: "*Preattribute annoying events and information about such events – to the extent possible – to motives and circumstances that make the induction of annoyance appear unintentional and nondeliberate, and . . . reattribute annoying events and information about such events in the same manner*" (p. 382; emphasis original).

Following senses of flooding and negative attributions, separation and divorce are inevitable (Gottman, 1994). Once people latch onto negative explanations for conflict that reflect characteristics of the partner, then increased distance and personal isolation is said to occur. One reason for increased distance and isolation concerns how negative attributions help a person defend him/herself. For example, once you believe that your partner is an egomaniac (which also explains his/her forgetting your anniversary), then you would likely want to create space between you and your partner. At the same time, one starts to reframe the history of the marriage. For instance, people might tell friends, "I should have seen this coming," "He only cares about his friends," and so forth.

Finally, divorce occurs (Gottman, 1994). As one might anticipate, given the general negative processes that are involved to get to this point, the divorce can be less than amicable. The important point to consider concerns how divorce is largely a function of how negative conflict tactics lead to perceptions, experiences, and attributions that in turn lead to increased distance, recasting of the marriage, and divorce.

Cultural Influences on Marital Conflict

An important point to make up front is that we see *all* family conflict processes as influenced by broad cultural factors (see figure 1.2). However, most family conflict research has been conducted with white (European origin) samples. Accordingly, generalizations based on findings from these studies inherently reflect orientations toward European American cultural values, such as individualism, directness, and equity. Our goal in providing this section and similar sections throughout the book is to direct the reader to important cultural issues and exceptions not apparent in studies conducted with primarily European American samples.

The lack of research on marital conflict outside of European American samples represents a surprising state of affairs considering the rise in cross-cultural marriages and immigration patterns that result in large minority populations in any given country (Cheng & Tardy, 2009; Wheeler et al., 2010). The few research studies that have targeted non-white populations tend to focus on either Asian-origin or Latino-origin couples (e.g., Bermúdez & Stinson, 2011; Cheng, 2010; Cheng & Tardy, 2009; Chuang & Su, 2009; Sandhya, 2009; Wheeler et al., 2010). We highlight compelling insights about cultural influences on marital conflict identified in studies of these two populations.

Asian Couples

Asian cultures often are influenced by Confucianism, which "emphasizes social harmony, clear lines of authority, and sacrificing individual needs for the sake of the needs of the group" (Chuang & Su, 2009, p. 527). Several researchers have predicted that these cultural values influence marital conflict processes to the degree that marital conflict would look very different in Asian marriages than they do in European American marriages (e.g., Cheng, 2010; Cheng & Tardy, 2009; Sandhya, 2009). For example, Cheng and Tardy (2009) examined the role of silence in conflict management processes, comparing Taiwanese, Chinese-American, and non-Asian American married couples. Non-Asian Americans in their study were more likely than Asians to use silence to protect their own self-image in marital conflict and they were also more likely than Chinese couples to use silence to control marital conflict. Cheng and Tardy also investigated the role of "self-construals" in their study of silence. Self-construals are personal views of how connected we feel to others. Although we all have interdependent (highly connected to others) and independent (fairly unconnected to others) self-construals, different cultures tend to emphasize interdependence over independence. Cheng and Tardy (2009) found that participants with interdependent self-construals are more likely to use silence to keep from embarrassing or hurting their partner in an argument and less likely to use silence to protect their own image. These findings seem to support the influence of American cultural values of self-interest and autonomy as well as the Asian values of collective interest and harmony in marital conflict processes.

However, the ways in which marital conflict associates with outcomes such as individual happiness and marital satisfaction seem to be very similar across cultures. Cheng (2010) studied a unique type of Taiwanese married couple, selecting only Taiwanese men who had married foreign women from Southeast Asia and China. These marriages were selected as representing highly traditional marriages with patriarchal structures and highly structured sex role expectations. Cheng (2010) found that even in these traditional, structured, and patriarchal marriages, both husbands and wives were more satisfied with their marriages when integrating, obliging, and compromising (as opposed to competing and avoiding) were used to manage marital conflicts. These findings reflect outcomes reported in non-traditional marriages as well. However, the role of obliging, in which one partner "gives in" to resolve the issue, might reflect a connection between the Asian cultural value of family harmony and marital satisfaction in these traditional marriages. Sandhya (2009) also found outcomes of marital conflict in Asian couples that mirror outcomes in European American couples. Sandhya's participants were married couples from urban India, with approximately two-thirds of couples being in arranged marriages. This study found that higher frequencies of conflicts in marriages were related to less happy participants and that the number of marital "good times" identified by participants was negatively correlated with the number of marital conflicts. In other words, long-term outcomes of marital conflict in these culturally specific marriage types are very similar to outcomes we discussed earlier in the chapter.

Latino Couples

The second cultural group that has garnered notable research attention is Latino couples. This group is of particular empirical interest considering that people of Latino origin, particularly from Mexico, represent the largest and fastest-growing ethnic minority population in the United States (Wheeler et al., 2010). Bermúdez and Stinson (2011) used Gottman's couple typology (see Kelley, 2012, for a description), which is similar to Fitzpatrick's typology we discussed earlier in the chapter, as the basis for developing a typology of Latino married couples. Bermúdez and Stinson (2011) argued that Gottman's and other typologies have been developed based on responses from primarily European American couples and unique qualities exist that need to be recognized in Latino couples.

Bermúdez and Stinson's research resulted in five couple types: (1) *United* couples share characteristics with Fitzpatrick's independent couples and Gottman's validating couples, reporting "feelings of togetherness and sharing, being best friends or companions, thinking positively about marital issues, feeling marital satisfaction, rarely arguing or disagreeing, and liking the way they communicate" (p. 77); (2) *Harmonious* couples are similar to Gottman's conflict-avoiding couples, reporting "acceptance of things in marriage they cannot change, lack of desire to talk about or analyze problems, especially when they disagree, and not wanting to share negative feelings or to be disrespectful" (p. 77); (3) *Conservative* couples also are conflict-avoidant and share similarities with Fitzpatrick's traditional couples, valuing religious values and beliefs and relying on traditional gender roles, beliefs, and traditional gender role scripts to solve problems in times of disagreement (p. 78); (4) *Autonomous* couples coincide with Fitzpatrick's separate couples, "valuing being separate individuals, often doing things separately, and wanting to have separate and different friends" (p. 78); and (5) *Passionate* couples are similar to Gottman's volatile couples, reporting "honestly confronting disagreements, comfort with strong expressions of negative feelings, understanding values through arguments, defending your views, enjoying to discuss diverse perspectives, and experiencing romance and jealously in the marriage" (p. 78).

Comparing these couple types across husbands, wives, birth country, and language preference, Bermúdez and Stinson (2011) found that most Latino husbands and wives reported using a *united* style in their marriage. However, when husbands were born in the United States, couples tended to report an *autonomous* marital type. Interestingly, when wives reported being bilingual, both husbands and wives reported being less *harmonious* and husbands reported being more *united*. Overall, this research is promising for taking a culturally sensitive approach to marital types, conflict, and communication.

Similarly, Wheeler et al. (2010) investigated how Mexican-origin couples handled marital conflict and how those processes related to marital satisfaction. Overall, they found that both husbands and wives used solution-oriented conflict strategies more than control or non-confrontation strategies. The authors argue that this finding is "consistent with the premise that Mexican-origin families often place an emphasis on group harmony and familism values and thus may endorse conflict resolution strategies that promote mutually satisfying conflict outcomes for both

members of the marital dyad" (Wheeler et al., 2010, p. 1001).
Wheeler et al. (2010) did find, however, that husbands used
more non-confrontation than wives and that wives used more
control than husbands. This finding comports with the demand–
withdraw pattern discussed earlier in the chapter. Additionally,
the researchers note that "Mexican-origin families often have
traditional gender-typed attitudes about family roles, and relationship maintenance often is a role of women . . . and thus they use
controlling strategies to manage conflicts" (p. 1001). Interestingly,
participants with a bicultural orientation reported using solution-
oriented strategies more often than participants who were not
bicultural, perhaps indicating marital benefits of cultural adaptation processes. Furthermore, participants reported higher levels
of satisfaction and love in their marriages when they used more
solution-oriented strategies but less non-confrontation or control
strategies. These findings comport with our earlier discussions
about long-term impacts of conflict behaviors in marriages.

Implications

This chapter discussed various factors connected to marital conflict. At the outset, we noted that marriage (and family) compels
members to become closer to each other. One might expect that
increased closeness would lead to fewer conflicts – but such is not
the case. This closeness and resulting interdependence actually
lead to more conflicts.

The connections between conflict communication and marital
satisfaction and stability are not always clear. This is not often
expected. For example, one might believe that communication
leads to understanding, which then leads to satisfaction. Not the
case. How satisfied married partners are with different communication behaviors varies according to couple types. The key here
concerns how both partners share in their blueprints for marriage.

Next, most people believe that depression reflects an individual
trait. After all, depression occurs in individuals, though it is often
not obvious. Marital conflict represents a crucible for mixing all

kinds of personal thoughts, feelings, and behaviors. Unexpectedly, we find support for a cyclical model of depression: Depression leads to negative conflict, which leads to depression.

Next, we considered how marital conflict relates to one's physical health. The reader might have believed that conflict communication has little to do with one's health. Now we sincerely hope those expectations are refuted by the data. Conflict communication is seriously connected to one's health, in terms of heart functions, hormones, and immune system. Knowing these facts should enable you to live longer – provided that you manage conflict in cooperative ways (table 2.1).

Gottman's model of divorce was discussed, and several unexpected elements emerge. One important element concerns how people make attributions for their partner's conflict behavior. Once people latch on to these negative attributions, divorce follows (at least, according to this model). The reader might not have expected that without positive attributions for conflict, there is no going back. Positive attributions are those that explain the conflict as stemming from something external to the partner ("The rain made him late"), unstable to the partner ("She got mad because she is under stress at work"), and specific to the conflict and not generalizable to other contexts ("He forgot Mother's Day but remembered my birthday").

Although cultural factors influence nuances of marital conflict processes and expectations in marriage relationships, research across cultures indicates that long-term impacts of marital conflict depend very much on *how* conflict is handled. Interestingly, married and domestic partners across cultures seem to value direct and cooperative approaches to marital conflict even when other approaches are present and culturally accepted.

The next chapter pans away from the marriage. It looks at the effects of marital conflict on the children, known as interparental conflict (IPC), post-divorce conflict, and how stepfamilies manage conflict.

3

Interparental Conflict, Post-Divorce, and Stepfamilies

Steve dropped his sons off at his ex-wife's apartment after his weekend with them. As he was saying his goodbyes to his sons he casually mentioned to his ex-wife, Hillary, "I can't take the boys for my scheduled Tuesday night this week. I'm traveling for work." Hillary flared in anger, "What?! I work Tuesday nights, which I specifically requested because those are your nights with the boys! What do you expect me to do with the boys Tuesday night when I work until 10:30?" Steve returned her glare, "I expect you to be home taking care of your children. You are their mother." Hillary retorted, "Oh, and just how am I supposed to pay rent and support myself and the boys if I don't work? We aren't married anymore. You can't call the shots like that anymore!" The boys, clearly unnerved by this exchange, quietly moved away from their mother and into the apartment. Hillary walked in and slammed the door.

As couples transition into parenthood, they take themselves with them. That is, their behaviors – including conflict strategies and tactics – do not change that much. Their patterns of conflict also can become solidified during parenthood. However, more than the marriage is at stake once children are born. The safety and well-being of the children directly depends on how well their parents get along. This chapter emphasizes how marital conflict and divorce affects children, followed by an extension of how stepfamilies operate and manage conflict.

Interparental Conflict

By way of preview, we want to indicate at the beginning that negative interparental conflict (IPC) adversely affects children, probably more so than divorce (Afifi et al., 2010; Amato & Keith, 1991; Rhoades, 2008). As the reader might anticipate, competitive and avoidant communication strategies have negative effects on children. For example, Jenkins and Smith (1991) found that parents' use of negative, hostile conflict positively connected to child behavioral and emotional problems. The authors concluded that "[hostile] conflict is the element in a disharmonious marriage which is most deleterious to children" (p. 805). And boys and girls learn how to manage conflict largely from their parents. Crockenberg and Langrock (2001), for example, found that six-year-olds mimicked the conflict behaviors of their same-sex parents.

Two qualifications precede this section. First, this section examines conflict between partners and its effect on children. It does not examine single-parent families simply because research on that topic is lacking. However, that is not to say that the ideas, findings, and theories covered below do not apply. Indeed, it would appear quite plausible to us that much of the following might occur in single-parent homes. Second, children's behavior also affects how parents behave toward each other, including their conflict messages (Schermerhorn et al., 2010). That is, parents are affected by children as children are affected by parents. However, 99 percent of the research leads us to examine interparental conflict effects on children. So we go there.

In this section, we examine how interparental conflict affects children. We discuss effects of IPC on children in terms of spillover from the marital relationship to the parent–child relationship, triangulation, children's appraisals of IPC, and emotional security.

Spillover

Spillover refers to "the direct transfer of mood, affect, or behavior from one setting to another" (Buehler & Gerard, 2002, p. 78).

Likewise, Krishnakumar and Buehler (2000) define spillover as "emotions, affect, and mood generated in the marital realm [that] transfers to the parent–child relationship" (p. 26). In terms of IPC, then, spillover highlights the *transfer* of marital conflict processes to the parent–child relationship. That is, a tendency exists for the parent to use negative or positive communication with the child as s/he does with the partner.

Particularly bothersome is how the negative emotions in marital interactions find their way into negative behaviors in the parent–child relationship (Crockenberg & Langrock, 2001; Krishnakumar & Buehler, 2000). More precisely, O'Donnell et al. (2010) argued that "the core tenet of the spillover hypothesis is that the emotional distress and distractions of IPC drain parental resources and make it less likely that parents will provide children with warmth, support, and structure, which in turn negatively impacts children's emotional well being" (p. 13). Fosco and Grych (2010) found that negative IPCs reduced the amount of closeness and increased conflicts between children and parents. The converse of this hypothesis is that one can provide warm, involved, and responsive parenting, which in turn buffers the effects of IPC (DeBoard-Lucas et al., 2010).

Increased harshness and lack of involvement/responsiveness are two common spillover parental behaviors (Webster-Stratton & Hammond, 1999). For example, Buehler and Gerard (2002) found that childhood maladjustment occurred as a result of parental spillover of negative conflict in terms of harsh parental discipline and lack of parental involvement (p. 88). In addition, given negative IPC, children tend to perceive their relationships with their parents as negative (Osborne & Fincham, 1996), or they perceive their parents as unavailable (Clark & Phares, 2004). Moreover, these perceptions of parental negativity and unavailability associate with child adjustment problems (e.g., internalizing and externalizing problems; Benson et al., 2008; Webster-Stratton & Hammond, 1999).

Yu et al. (2010) found that both marital conflict and divorce adversely affected parent–adult child relationships. In addition, whether someone was divorced or not affected the negativity in conflict. More precisely, Yu et al. (2010) found that intact family partners showed *greater* negativity than did those who were divorced. These authors argued that although divorce is a stressful event for children, ongoing negative conflicts are even more stressful and therefore more dysfunctional.

Conflict behaviors in IPC are likely transmitted, and thereby learned, by children. Crockenberg and Langrock (2001) found that six-year-olds mimicked the behaviors of their same-sexed parents. In a direct test of the transmission hypothesis, Van Doorn et al. (2007) argued that, "The extent to which adolescents use [various conflict tactics] with their parents might depend on the extent to which parents use these conflict resolution styles in their marital relationship" (p. 426). Van Doorn et al. found support for the transmission hypothesis. In particular, IPC engagement (e.g., "getting furious and losing my temper") and problem-solving (e.g., "compromising and discussion") led to parent–adolescent engagement and problem-solving two years later. (However, no transmission effects were found for withdrawal [e.g., "not listening and refusing to discuss the issue"].) Likewise, Cue et al. (2008) found that young adult children's relational quality depended on their conflict behaviors, which were affected by their parents' conflict behaviors. These findings imply an intergeneration transmission of conflict management behaviors.

Triangulation

Triangulation "generally reflects an interaction pattern in which children become involved in their parents' conflict or feel pressure to side with one parent against the other" (Grych et al., 2004, p. 650). In most cases, triangulation reflects a lack of appropriate boundaries between the parent's role and the child's role, which can lead to child confusion and dismay (Grych et al., 2004; Robin and Foster, 1989). Approximately one-third of children are occasionally caught in the middle between their parents in conflict and they tend to be female (Amato & Afifi, 2006; Buchanan et al., 1991). As might be expected, children whose parents engage in negative, competitive conflict are more likely to feel caught between parents than are those in homes where their parents engage in cooperative communication (Amato & Afifi, 2006; Buchanan et al., 1991; Grych et al., 2004). For example, Buchanan et al. (1991) found that feeling caught was highest for children with "conflicted" parents, then "disengaged" parents, and then "cooperative" parents.

Several effects of triangulation on children have been discovered. For example, children tend to blame themselves for their parent's conflict if they are triangulated (Fosco & Grych, 2010). Importantly, triangulation mediates, or connects, the effect of IPC on child adjustment. In other words, IPC appears to first affect triangulation which then, in turn, affects the child's adjustment. For example, Grych et al. (2004) found that triangulation explained the effects of IPC on adolescents' adjustment. They found that triangulation itself led to both internalizing (e.g., withdrawal) and externalizing (e.g., aggression) problems in adolescents. Also, Buchanan et al. (1991) found that triangulation mediated the effects of marital discord on adolescent depression and deviance. Depression and deviance both correspond to internalizing and externalizing problems.

One critical factor in IPC concerns the extent to which the partners support each other's parental attempts. Shimkowski and Schrodt (2012) argued that partners can undermine each other's parenting or endorse it. They found that affectively endorsing each other's coparenting reduced the negative effects of the demand–withdraw pattern on their young adult children's self-esteem. In a similar vein, Grych et al. (2004) found that the closeness of the family served a protective function against triangulation. It appears that coparenting works against triangulation and helps lead to more functional outcomes for the children.

Appraisals

Appraisals refer to evaluations of whether and how particular events relate to one's well-being (Maguire, 2012, p. 52). IPCs certainly constitute particular events that children see as having a direct influence on their well-being. As Grych and Fincham (1990) stated, IPC raises three questions for children: "What is happening?," "Why is it happening?," "What can I do about it?" (p. 281). Appraisals are the first set of processes in answering these questions. In this light, Crockenberg and Langrock (2001) observed that children use IPC for information that provides meaning about their own personal goals, for example, whether they are loved, protected, and will enjoy future interactions with parents. Davies and Cummings (1998) argued that emotional security "motivates children's actions and reactions" (p. 125).

Two appraisals are especially important, according to Grych, Fosco, and colleagues – threat and self-blame (e.g., Fosco & Grych, 2007, 2010; Grych et al., 2004). *Threat* refers to the extent that the child feels threatened, the parent–child relationship is in jeopardy, that the IPC will escalate, and other concerns. *Self-blame* appraisals concern whether the child feels responsible for the IPC, for example, as having even been born or whether the IPC is about him/her. As one can predict, these two appraisals are fundamentally damning. The more children believe that their parents' conflicts threaten their well-being and are their fault, the more the IPCs will be salient and affect the children negatively.

Two processes are at work here. First, and again, negative and competitive IPC leads to appraisals of threat and self-blame (e.g., Grych et al., 2004). In particular, the more frequent, intense, and irrational the conflicts, the more likely they affect appraisals in a negative way. For example, Fosco and Grych (2010) found that intense and poorly managed conflicts increased the child's sense of threat, self-blame, and inability to cope with the parent's conflicts.

Second, these negative appraisals then directly lead to child maladjustment. For example, Grych et al. (2004) found that perceived threat in particular filtered the association between IPC intensity and child internal adjustment problems. Threat appraisals in this study concerned whether the parents might divorce, the child might be drawn into the conflict, and so forth. In Atkinson et al. (2009), four types of threat filtered the effects of IPC on internalizing problems: fear of conflict escalation; fear of being drawn into the conflict; fear of family breakdown; and fear of a disruption in the parent–child relationship. In addition, Grych et al. (2004) found effects for self-blame appraisals. Here self-blame also filtered the effects of IPC on internal adjustment problems (though not as strongly as did threat appraisals). Some children are more positive and resilient, to be sure. For example, O'Donnell et al. (2010) found that children with a negative cognitive style were more likely than children with a positive cognitive style to engage in threat and self-blame appraisals. But, in general, appraisals of threat and self-blame powerfully affect how much IPCs affect children.

Emotional Security Theory

One important explanation for the IPC processes of spillover, triangulation, and appraisals is *emotional security theory* (Cummings & Davies, 2010). According to Davies and Cummings (1998), the emotional security hypothesis "posits that preserving and promoting [children's] own sense of emotional security is a primary *goal* that motivates children's actions and reactions" (p. 125). It holds that IPC is filtered by the child's sense of emotional security before IPC affects childhood adjustment (Davies & Cummings, 1998). Accordingly, the fear, resentment, threat, and self-blame that might accompany IPC depends on whether or not the child feels safe.

Figure 3.1 presents the causal model that Cummings and Davies offer to indicate the links among IPC and children's adjustment problems. First, the theory begins with an emphasis on the destructive (not constructive) forms of IPC (far left). More positive and direct forms of IPC are not believed to negatively affect children's sense of security.

Second, and within the larger context of family characteristics, destructive conflict messages affect the child's sense of security (or interparental insecurity). In terms of (in)security, Cummings and Davies (2010) note that the "'set goal' of emotional security regulates and is regulated by at least three domains of regulatory response patterns: emotional reactivity, regulation of exposure to conflict, and internal representations" (pp. 33–4). Emotional reactivity involves such emotions as ongoing fear, vigilance, and distress. Behavioral regulation includes the child's attempts to

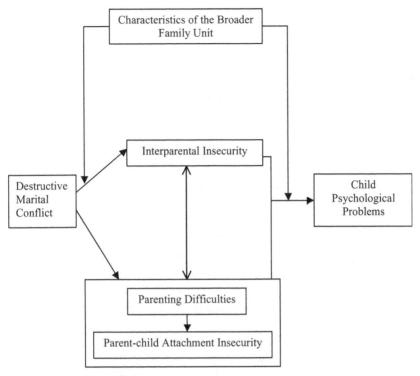

Figure 3.1 Emotional Security Theory Paths Involving Interparental Conflict

Source: Cummings and Davies (2010), p. 31.

become involved in the conflict or take some other behavioral option. Finally, internal representations represent how the child makes sense of his or her parent's conflicts, including expectations for the future. Cummings and Davies also report several studies showing that children become *more* emotionally sensitive, or *sensitized*, to destructive conflicts as they reoccur. They pointed out that the reason children do not become habituated to IPC is because they always have a need to feel secure; indeed, increased frequency of IPC leads to higher emotional arousal in children because it continually and negatively affects their sense of well-being.

Third, figure 3.1 indicates that a combination of destructive conflict and insecurity lead to two areas of problems in the parent–child relationship. The first area concerns parenting difficulties. These difficulties reflect those mentioned under the spillover section above. Decreases in warmth, involvement, and acceptance are also salient here (p. 108). The second problem area concerns how destructive conflicts harm the married partners' attachment systems (pp. 111–12). Adult attachment theory concerns how adults form attachments based on their mental models of how relationships work. If married partners "learn" from their hostile conflicts not to trust others, to show warmth, or to support others, they are less likely to show positive models for how relationships work to their children.

Finally, emotional security theory predicts that the combination of interparental insecurity and parenting problems affect children's adjustment (far right). If parents can demonstrate warm, supportive, and involved behaviors, then the effects due to insecurity are minimized, for example. Of course, the theory also suggests that the effects due to warm and supportive parenting are lessened by insecurity.

Research of this theory has been largely supportive. For example, Du Rocher Schudlich and Cummings (2007) examined how children's emotional security regarding IPC affected children's adjustment problems. Parents engaged in videotaped conflict interactions that their children later watched. These authors found that parental depression affected children's emotional security which then affected their adjustment. Likewise, Kouros et al. (2008) examined how parental depression is linked to children's internalizing problems of depression and anxiety. As anticipated, marital conflict (especially when parents were depressed) negatively affected children's security, which, in turn, affected their own depression. According to Cummings and Davies (2010):

> [E]motional security can be thought of as a bridge between the child and the world. When the marital relationship is high-functioning, a secure base is provided for the child. Like a structurally sound bridge, a positive marital relationship supports the child's optimal functioning in the context of potentially threatening conditions, fostering explora-

tion and confident relationships with others. When destructive marital conflict damages the bridge, the child may become hesitant to move forward and lack confidence, or may move forward in a dysfunctional way, failing to find the best footing in relations with others or within the self. (p. 35)

Post-Divorce Families

Many people lament how high the divorce rate has become – in the US approximately 40–50 percent of married couples divorce (Teachman et al., 2006). In many or perhaps most cases, divorce can reflect a marriage that became dysfunctional for one or both partners (Gottman, 1994). Whether or not divorce is a good–bad, right–wrong decision is not the purpose of this book. Instead, we turn our attention to how divorce affects individual family members and the prospect of future families. Naturally, we find that how people manage conflicts interacts with divorce to affect both individual and relational consequences.

Individual Consequences of Divorce

Interparental conflict (IPC) remains an important factor when discussing the effects of divorce. Buchanan and Heiges (2001) reviewed the research on IPC after divorce. Four relevant observations are discussed here. First, IPC is more likely to be intense immediately after the divorce. That is, only about 10–20 percent of divorced couples engage in highly intense and confrontational conflict. After the first one to two years, conflicts tend to subside both in terms of frequency and intensity. Over time, former partners tend to rely more on avoidant conflict strategies (Buchanan & Heiges, 2001). Second, the topics of conflict revolve around the children as well as around economic stress (such as the vignette at the beginning of this chapter). Salient conflict topics involve child visitation and custody rights, child discipline, children's adjustment to divorce, and the divorced partner's intimate relations with other people (Buchanan & Heiges, 2001). Third, the effects of divorce on children likely vary as a function of time – with more severe effects occurring during the early phase of the divorce. Buchanan and Heiges argued the following:

> the impact of conflict differs by family structure at certain times or on certain types of outcomes. For example, it is possible that interparental conflict has a stronger impact on parenting and child adjustment in divorced as compared to nondivorced families, but only in the immediate aftermath of the divorce. Perhaps after more time has passed and the frequency and intensity of conflict diminish, the differential impact disappears. (p. 347)

Finally, Buchanan and Heiges documented how parents can individually affect the negative impacts of divorce. Such effects can be positive, for example, when the mother develops a strong bond, or negative, for example, when parents attempt to win the loyalties of their children and so triangulate them (Afifi & Schrodt, 2003a). Accordingly, how parents communicate with their children can strongly affect the impacts of post-divorce conflict.

The concrete effects of divorce on children should not be dismissed. Research has found that divorce affects the well-being and adjustment of children (for a review, see Segrin et al., 2005). For example, in his meta-analysis, Amato (2001) found that children from divorced homes had poorer academic achievement, more conduct problems, lower psychological adjustment, poorer self-esteem, and worse social relationships. In an 11-year longitudinal study, Ge et al. (2006) found that depression was affected by divorce – with depression increasing from the 9th grade through adolescence, and then declining around the age of 20. Girls, more than boys, showed increased depression due to divorce.

These effects, however, depend on how much conflict is in the home. Amato and Keith (1991) found that children in high-conflict homes were worse off than children of divorce. Moreover, children from divorced homes where the parents did not engage in intense and negative conflict behaviors were better off than children from divorced homes where the parents engaged in negative conflict tactics. Amato (2001) found that when marital conflict is "overt, intense, chronic, and unresolved, then children are better off if a divorce occurs; when marital conflict is absent, then children are better off in intact homes" (p. 357). Morris and West (2001) concluded that "[O]verall, it appears that children have better adjustment if the parental conflict ends with the divorce rather than being extended into the coparental relationship" (p. 95).

Relational Consequences of Divorce

Divorce also negatively affects the relationships children have in the future. First, children of divorce are much more likely to get divorced themselves. This finding is known as the *intergenerational transmission* of divorce. Cui and Fincham (2010) indicated that the "intergenerational transmission of divorce is now well documented" (p. 331). For example, Amato and DeBoer (2001) found that divorce (more so than conflict) predicted the child's divorce in the future. Moreover, Teachman et al. (2006) concluded, "The long-term upward trend in divorce does not suggest the likelihood of a return to more conservative attitudes toward divorce. To the contrary, attitudes toward divorce are likely to remain quite accepting" (p. 71).

Second, divorce jeopardizes the quality of children's future romantic involvements. Segrin et al. (2005) reported that divorce was associated with the adult child's higher family conflict, negative attitudes toward marriage, and less likelihood of being in a close relationship. And higher family conflict connects to difficulty managing relationships in the future. Riggio (2004) stated that young adults from high-conflict divorced homes "may have difficulty forming stable, satisfying relationships" (p. 100). Herzog and Cooney (2002) reported that parental divorce led to poorer communication competence and intimate communication with a partner years later.

Importantly, *the combination* of divorce and negative marital conflict affect the child's future romantic relationships. Cui and Fincham (2010) found that divorce led to the adult child's negative attitudes toward marriage, which led to decreased commitment to one's partner, which then led to decreased satisfaction with the relationship. At the same time, frequent, intense, and unresolved interparental conflict led to the adult child's current relational conflict, which led to decreased relational satisfaction. To summarize these findings rather simply: divorce leads to poor relational quality through fear of commitment, whereas negative IPC leads to poor relational quality though the learning of poor conflict management skills.

Some research has found that the relational effects from divorce differ according to the child's biological sex. For example, Jacquet and Surra (2001) found that women from divorced homes formed less relational trust and satisfaction. Also, women from divorced homes reported more ambivalence (i.e., need for affection combined with fear of abandonment) and conflict. Interestingly, women from divorced homes also reported more involvement in passionate love (but not friendship-based love). Men from divorced (vs. intact) homes did not report these differences. However, men from divorced (vs. intact) homes did differ on the variables of trust and conflict if their partners' parents were divorced. In other words, the women's parents' marital status affected both partners. Similarly, Amato and DeBoer (2001) found that if the wife's parents had been divorced, the likelihood of marital disruption increases by 70 percent.

The effects of divorce on the parent–child relationship also merit discussion. Afifi and Schrodt (2003a) examined both adolescents and young adults from divorced or intact homes. They wanted to predict how much these participants avoided discussion of family issues and how satisfied they were with their parents. Afifi and Schrodt found that participants from divorced homes (vs. non-divorced homes) felt less close to their parents, perceived their parents to be less communicatively competent, saw more demand–withdraw conflict tactics, and had greater feelings of being caught between parents. Moreover, children of divorce had higher avoidance but lower satisfaction scores. However, these effects due to divorce – which were quite substantial – were lessened if the child viewed the parent as communicatively competent and did not feel caught in the middle. Afifi and Schrodt concluded, "the parents' communication skills and the extent to which children feel as if they must ameliorate their parents' disputes may account for a more complete explanation of children's avoidance and dissatisfaction with their parents than the divorce itself" (2003a, p. 166). Likewise, Riggio (2004) found that high conflict homes involved less affection with parents, less independence from parents, and lower emotional support from parents than did low conflict homes.

In a follow-up study, Schrodt and Afifi (2007) examined how demand/withdraw, aggressive communication, and negative self-disclosure (e.g., a parent's disclosure about the other parent) affected children's feeling caught in the middle, which in turn, affected family satisfaction and mental health in both intact and divorced families. They found that feeling caught in the middle was positively and strongly associated with demand/withdraw and aggressive communication; and it was moderately associated with inappropriate parental disclosures. Also, family satisfaction and mental health were negatively associated with demand/withdraw and aggressive communication, but not parental negative disclosure. Next, time since divorce was inversely linked to all three negative communication behaviors and with feeling caught; time since divorce was positively linked to family satisfaction. These findings indicate that time heals. Finally, demand/withdraw and aggressive communication predicted feelings of being caught in the middle depending on divorce status and whether or not the relationship was close. Whether or not the relationship was close mattered more in nondivorced families. For example, in nondivorced families, aggressive communication predicted feeling caught for those in low close families versus high close families. So being close in nondivorced families was tied to lower aggressiveness. The authors argued that we cannot simply look at close versus not close families; we should distinguish their contexts, in this instance, whether or not the family is divorced.

One important sex difference exists regarding the parent–child relationship: Divorce tends to have more negative effects for fathers than mothers. For instance, Riggio (2004) found that divorce led to more negative assessments of the father but more positive assessments of the mother. Likewise, Frank (2007) found that mothers' relationships with their children were positively affected by divorce, whereas fathers' relationships – especially with their daughters – were negatively affected by divorce. Frank's results "confirm a prevalent finding that the father–child relationship is particularly vulnerable to divorce" (p. 117). A few reasons for this parental sex difference emerge (Frank, 2007, p. 119). One is simply due to the fact that mothers have sole or primary custody of the children in the vast majority of cases, so the frequency of mother–child interactions remain intact or even increase post-divorce. A second reason is that children see the pain and effort that mothers exert as a single parent and so come to respect them more. As Riggio (2004) put it, mothers and children must "struggle to adapt to changes accompanying divorce" (p. 109).

Stepfamilies

As the reader can imagine, stepfamily conflict can occur quite a bit. This section first discusses the climate of a stepfamily household followed by conflict topics and conflict management strategies.

The Stepfamily Climate

A *stepfamily* refers to a family "in which at least one of the adults has a child (or children) from a previous relationship" (Ganong & Coleman, 2004, p. 2). Approximately 50 percent of all marriages in the US are remarriages and, of these, 25 percent bring in children from a previous marriage (Ganong & Coleman, 2004). The stepfamily is more complex than intact families (i.e., with both biological parents) (Fine, 2001). For example, it is possible to have the mother, stepfather, father, children and stepchildren all involved in defining the family.

Moreover, the roles and rights of the stepparent are often ambiguous (Fine, 2001). For example, Schmeeckle et al. (2006) found that only about one-third of their participants viewed the stepfather as a parent (though a majority saw their stepparent as "fully" or "quite a bit" a family member). How the stepparent fits into the family – as a family member who is not a legitimate parent – reflects a problematic environment that has implications for how biologically related family members relate to each other and to the stepparents (typically stepfathers). Consider the important role of who disciplines the children. Cartwright (2010) found that 77 percent of people discipline their own children, 25 percent of stepfamilies shared the discipline, and only 1.5 percent said that the stepparent disciplined the children. No doubt the disparity in these figures shows a probable conflict topic (e.g., the stepparent wanting more say regarding discipline or the parent wanting less control over disciplining behaviors). Stepfamilies also contain more uncertainty and avoidance of topics, at least in the first few years of their existence (Afifi & Schrodt, 2003b; Golish & Caughlin, 2002). And they are more stressful, in part because they contain a lack of role clarity for its members (Johnson et al., 2008).

Parental styles also differ between stepfamilies and intact families. For example, Hetherington and Jodl (1994) analyzed three longitudinal data sets that compared children from intact homes to stepfamilies. They compared three types of parenting types: *authoritative*, which involved warmth, low negativity, monitoring, and moderate control; *disengaged*, which included moderate negativity, low monitoring, low control, and low positivity; and *authoritarian*, which comprised high levels of conflict, monitoring, control attempts, and little positivity. Here is what they found:

Overall, biological fathers tended to use more authoritative parenting style; stepfathers tended to rely on disengaged behaviors. Counter to the stereotype of the mean stepparent, stepfathers were not more likely to engage in authoritarian behaviors. The disengaged style of the stepparent remained over time, even once the family became stable – that is, there was no noticeable increase in positivity, warmth, or disciplinary action. Over time, the stepchild eschews attempts by the stepparent to develop a close relationship, and the stepparent responds. In describing this general trend, Hetherington and Jodl (1994) stated:

Early attempts to establish a positive stepfather–child relationship through self-disclosure, common interests, and shared activities were typically met with highly coercive reactions from stepchildren. Despite this resistance on the part of the stepchildren, and in spite of expressing concerns about the lack of feelings of closeness or rapport with stepchildren, many stepfathers spent time with their stepchildren and remained relatively open to their stepchildren in the early stages of remarriage. Over time, however, the majority of stepfathers no longer attempted to engage in a warm and supportive relationship with their stepchildren as a result of continued resistance or distancing behavior, as well as the persistence of problem behaviors among stepchildren. (pp. 65–6)

Likewise, Kurdek and Fine (1993) found that adolescents perceived their stepparents as more permissive than did adolescents living with both biological parents. Kurdek and Fine also reported that adolescents in intact homes perceived more parental warmth and less conflict than adolescents living with stepparents.

One set of related findings regarding stepfamilies concerns how well adjusted the children become in them. Two studies that summarized previous research on the topic are relevant. First, Amato (1994) conducted a meta-analysis that compared several indicators of well-being between stepchildren and children from intact homes. Amato found that stepchildren differed from children in intact families on several measures, but only weakly so. This means that most stepchildren are similar to children in intact families. Nevertheless, Amato found that children in intact families had better scores for the following variables: academic achievement, conduct/behavior problems, psychological adjustment, self-esteem, and functional relationships. In a similar manner, Ganong and Coleman (1993) performed a meta-analysis examining self-esteem and behavioral differences between children in intact families and children in stepfamilies and single-parent families. They found that children in intact homes had slightly higher self-esteem, substantively lower internal behavioral problems (e.g, depression), and slightly lower external behavioral problems (e.g., fighting) than did stepchildren. Stepchildren had higher self-esteem than did single-parent children. These findings indicate that children in stepfamilies might have a tougher time than children in intact families, but they fare better than children with single parents (cf. Hanson et al., 1996).

Importantly, however, not all stepfamilies are alike. Bray and Kelly (1998) reported on three types of stepfamilies: *neotraditionalist*, *matriarchal*, and *romantic* marriages. The neotraditional stepfamily marriage creates an appropriate parental role for the stepfather, distinguishes the current marriage from the former, effectively manages change, and coordinates how to deal with ex-spouses. The matriarchal stepfamily marriage is signified by the mother's control over the household, including parenting. Finally, the romantic stepfamily marriage lacks the properties of the neotraditional marriage but clings onto romantic (though sometimes unrealistic) ideals of marriage. Regardless of stepfamily marriage type, Bray and Kelly reported that strong stepfamilies have three foundations:

> First, the husband and wife have to attend to their adult needs – to nurture their relationship. Second, they need to develop a shared vision of marriage and family life. And third, they have to develop a consensus on parenting and other child-related issues. This consensus may vary depending on the type of stepfamily that the couple forms, but the *bottom line is that they have to agree on how to deal with the child*. (1998, p. 42, *emphasis original*)

On this last point, however, Cartwright (2010) reported that only 41 percent of remarried couples talked about how to raise the children early on, and 46 percent said that they coordinated how they would coparent as issues arose.

Schrodt (2006) also investigated whether stepfamilies differ from each other on the basis of dimensions relevant to family life. He found five types of stepfamilies: *bonded*, *functional*, *ambivalent*, *evasive*, and *conflictual*. The bonded stepfamilies were typified by high cohesion, low dissension, low avoidance, high involvement, high flexibility, and high expressiveness. Functional stepfamilies had many of the attributes of the bonded type, but functional stepfamilies were slightly less involved and expressive, and slightly more avoidant. The ambivalent stepfamily had near average scores on all the above dimensions. Evasive stepfamilies were characterized by higher levels of avoidance and dissension, and lower levels of involvement and flexibility. Finally, conflictual stepfamilies (as the name suggests) endorsed greater dissension and avoidance, an absence of family unity, and aversion to spending time together. Schrodt (2006) reported that "taken as a whole, bonded and functional stepfamilies were viewed as more [communicatively] competent, better functioning stepfamilies than those classified as ambivalent, evasive, and conflictual" (p. 329). Fortunately, most of the stepfamilies in this study were either bonded or functional.

Moreover, Schmeeckle et al. (2006) found that stepparents were more likely to be considered a member of the family if normative, structural, and associational solidarities were increased. In other words, if the stepchildren buy into the family roles, live nearby, and maintain a lot of contact with the parent/stepparent, then the stepparent was more likely to be perceived as a member of the family. This study suggests that the findings that compare stepfamilies to intact homes can differ depending on how much stepfamily members increase their solidarities.

Conflict Issues in Stepfamilies

Conflict issues in stepfamilies reflect their problematic environments. Fine's (2001) analysis yielded seven potential conflict issues. First, parents and stepparents might differ on parenting styles, with children also viewing their stepparents more as friends and less as parents.

Second, stepfamilies tend to contain more direct expressions of criticism and anger. Yet, more avoidance and withdrawal can occur in stepfamilies (e.g., Afifi & Schrodt, 2003b), which can lead to conflict. The reader should know that direct expression of anger and avoidance are not mutually exclusive – in fact, they can co-exist quite well in dysfunctional homes.

Third, the biological parent can feel divided loyalties between his/her children and his/her new marital partner. Parents might feel a primary alliance with their children and feel torn as to the extent of their exclusion of their marital partner who also deserves support and attention. Weaver and Coleman (2010) reported that role conflicts negatively affect mothers who feel caught in the middle, although mothers tend to side with their children. Likewise, Coleman et al. (2001) noted that the biological parent might adopt a "guard and protect" stance against the stepparent, especially when the child is harshly judged or slighted.

Fourth, Fine noted how boundary issues affected the step-family, for example, when the children challenge the stepparent. Boundary issues are critically important to stepfamilies, so we elaborate on these below.

The final four reasons are rather straightforward. Fifth, the child might play the parents and stepparents off each other. Sixth, differences exist between the marital partners regarding how much money should be spent on the children, with stepparents less willing to spend a lot of money. Seventh, conflicts can occur that involve the non-residential parent. Consider the following example (from Coleman et al., 2001, p. 65):

> I guess when Eric [my stepfather] tries to discipline or tries to provide input my dad gets mad. You know, he tries to say that [Eric] doesn't have any authority in the family – he shouldn't have any say in what happens between us kids. So that causes friction for me because I'm put in the middle because you can't take sides. They both talk about each other and tell you stuff so-like when they're in fights and mad at each other my mom will tell me stuff about my dad and my dad will tell me stuff about my mom.

Also, unresolved conflicts from the previous marriage can spread through the stepfamily (Afifi, 2003, p. 733). Finally, conflict can be acute between stepsiblings, often due to feelings of being unfairly treated (i.e., favoritism).

As mentioned, boundaries represent a primary conflict issue in stepfamilies. Coleman et al. (2001) found that the "nego-tiation of family boundaries was at the root" of most stepfamily conflicts (p. 59). They identified four conflict topics that present places where boundaries are contested: *resources* over posses-sions, space, privacy, time/attention, and finances; *loyalty* (often the mothers caught between her child and her husband); *"guard and protect"* issues (e.g., where the mother protects the child from the stepfather or the noncustodial parent); and *extended family member* conflicts (e.g., disagreements with new in-laws about how to raise the children). Similarly, Golish (2003) reported seven "challenges" that stepfamilies faced, most of which "involved negotiating boundaries" (p. 72): (1) feeling caught between stepfamily members (both stepchildren and parents experienced this); (2) managing boundaries with the noncustodial parent; (3) ambiguity of parental roles; (4) "traumatic bonding" (where mothers and children survived divorce and financial hardship); (5) vying for resources, such as money and space; (6) differences in conflict management styles; and (7) building solidarity as a family unit. In brief, stepfamilies have conflicts regarding the rules about family members' behaviors and roles.

Avoidance provides one clear way that boundaries can be established. Golish and Caughlin (2002) argued that "Stepchildren might want a relatively impermeable communication boundary between themselves and new stepfamily members. Thus, stepchildren may be likely to restrict the amount of private information that they share with their new steprelations" (p. 80). In fact, Golish and Caughlin found that children avoided their stepparents the most, followed by their biological fathers and then their biological mothers. Stepparents were most avoided in terms of discussing sexual issues, relationships, negative experiences, and dating. One possible goal with avoidance is simply to freeze out the stepparent from enjoying personal connection with the child.

A separate line of inquiry into the nature of stepfamilies comes from a dialectical perspective (e.g., Braithwaite et al., 2008). In this view, people are said to experience tensions that arise from the existence of mutually necessary but opposing contradictions (Baxter & Montgomery, 1996). For example, Baxter et al. (2004) found three underlying contradictions of the stepparent–stepchild relationship. These are *integration* (closeness–distance), *parental status* (legitimate–illegitimate), and *expression* (candor–discretion). In terms of integration, stepchildren reported being distant but also feeling close with (or a desire to feel close with) the stepparent. Contradictions involving parental status meant that the child wants to both recognize and refute the legitimacy of the stepparent's parental role. Contradictions about expression concerned how children wanted to discuss issues with the stepparent but exercised discretion in not doing so. Using dialectical theory, Braithwaite et al. (2008) reported a primary dialectical tension of *freedom–constraint*, or the freedom to communicate with parents but manage the constraints resulting from parental communication. Braithwaite et al. also reported two "radiants" of this dialectical contradiction: *openness–closedness* (e.g., navigating child–stepparent openness) and *control–restraint* (e.g., the stepchild having control over who the parent dates but not wanting to feel constrained to say what she or he really feels). In brief, the dialectical perspective provides an alternative view of the conflict issues at stake in stepfamilies.

It is clear that the amount of avoidance in a stepfamily constitutes a conflict problem as well as one way for children to establish clear boundaries (Golish & Caughlin, 2002). When children experience turmoil in the family, however, they need to discuss it (Dunn et al., 2001). Dunn et al. found that adolescents turn to friends as confidants. They also found that confiding in a parent was less frequent in father stepfamilies than in non-stepfamilies or stepmother-complex families (i.e., where both parents brought children from previous relationships). Confiding in the mother was less frequent in stepmother-complex families more so than in non-stepfamilies. Yet, Schrodt et al. (2008) found that stepparent families who share everyday talk were much more likely to be satisfied with each others' relationship. And the positive effects of everyday talk were due to the stepfather proclivities to share and the unique nature of the relationships between family members. Accordingly, in some stepfamilies, the sharing of information appears to be more valued than in others.

Managing Stepfamily Conflict

To our knowledge, only a handful of researchers have examined ways that people communicatively respond to stepfamily conflict. This section briefly reviews that material.

Table 3.1 Strategies for Managing Stepfamily Conflict

1. Compromising on rules/discipline, or parent disciplines
2. Presenting united parental front on rules/discipline
3. Talking *to* the person with whom one is in conflict
4. Child is out of home/spending time apart from family (child leaves voluntarily or is evicted)
5. Letting time take its course
6. Reframing the problem as less serious or family joke
7. Withdrawal (avoiding conflict)
8. Professional counseling
9. Moving (to larger or neutral space)
10. Family meetings
11. Mediating the disputes of others
12. Setting ultimatums
13. Spending leisure time together (e.g., vacations)

Source: Coleman et al. (2001), p. 60

Coleman et al. (2001) were perhaps the first to uncover the kinds of communication strategies that stepfamily members use to manage their conflicts. Table 3.1 presents the strategies found by Coleman et al. (2001). These authors found that the most used conflict management strategies were compromising, followed by a united parental front, talking to the person, child out of home, letting time take its course, reframing the problem, and then the rest. Coleman et al. noted that these conflict strategies likely vary in their effectiveness. The issue concerns how well each of these strategies function in different types of stepfamilies. For instance, talking to the person would appear to be most effective in bonded and functional families and least effective in evasive families (Schrodt, 2006).

Afifi (2003) noted that two kinds of communicative responses represented boundary separation in dysfunctional stepfamilies: over-privileging avoidance and competitive symmetry. *Overprivileging avoidance* means that avoidance "often became the standard rather than the exception" in dysfunctional stepfamilies. For instance, stepparents are avoided more than biological parents when it comes to talking about sexual issues, relationships, negative experiences, and dating (Golish & Caughlin, 2002). *Competitive symmetry* refers to how two people battle for control. Here is one example of competitive symmetry from Afifi (2003, p. 748):

> He [stepson] likes to be in control, and in . . . doesn't like to be told what to do. We had a physical confrontation and actually broke a pair of glasses over it. It was a rough time, but he actually just stood there in my face and said, "come on, come on hit me," very defiant.

Also, Afifi (2003) found four parental responses to boundary tensions in stepfamilies that appear to be more functional:

1. *openness and direct confrontation*, including metacommunication (i.e., communication about their communication);
2. *communicating a united front*, by enforcing rules together and not allowing alliances to form between the children and either parent;
3. *creating a positive image of the other parent*, for example, by not talking down about him or her; and
4. *minimizing*, or limiting contact with the other parent and not having conversations about the children when they are present.

An example of openness and direct confrontation in response to feeling caught is described by a mother (from Afifi, 2003, p. 744):

> There would be a conflict between Samantha and John [stepparent] or Matt and John, and they would both be coming to me and complaining about each other. You can't allow yourself to be caught in that trap and that you step back and say, "OK, you two need to talk to each other," but it was so easy to get sucked into it, to recognize that you were in that situation, and all of a sudden it would be "oh, this is it." Then I would say, "OK John, you need to go talk to Samantha."

Golish (2003) found that particular responses to her seven challenges mentioned on p. 72 were more functional than not. Stepfamilies with difficulties relied more on distancing, avoidance, and aggressiveness. Strong stepfamilies, however, engaged in more openness, inclusiveness, and positive maintenance behaviors. Moreover, Golish found that different challenges lead to different use of communication strategies. On the challenge of different conflict styles, for instance, being confrontational and avoidant were ineffective (recall these also lead to further conflicts, as noted above). Softening one's confrontational voice, being open and honest, and showing support were effective for strong stepfamilies (p. 68). On the challenge of resources, strong stepfamilies relied on openness, family meetings, and compromise (p. 67). On the issue of solidarity, strong families built it through openness, humor, and co-constructing a definition of "family" (pp. 69–70).

Cultural Influences

Not many studies have empirically examined cultural influences on interparental, post-divorce, and stepfamily conflict (McLoyd et al., 2001). The few studies have focused exclusively on interparental conflict rather than post-divorce or stepfamily conflict. Accordingly, we discuss here key insights gleaned from those studies and how we might move forward with attending to cultural influences on IPC, post-divorce, and stepfamily conflict.

The Attenuation Hypothesis

At the turn of the twenty-first century, McLoyd et al. (2001) reviewed the sparse research landscape of cultural comparisons of IPC, concluding that ethnic minority children in the US, "like majority children, respond to family and interparental conflict with increased psychological distress and lower levels of psychosocial and academic competence" (p. 109). However, they conjectured that ethnic minority children in general might be less vulnerable to the harmful effects of IPC than non-Hispanic white children due to an "attenuation effect." In essence, the attenuation effect predicts that the detrimental outcomes of IPC are lessened in ethnic minority children because they live in strong extended family networks and because they experience other "ethnic- and race-related stressful events and ongoing conditions" (McLoyd et al., 2001, p. 110) that overshadow effects from IPC. However, research published in the past several years does not support this prediction.

Recent research points to a consistent pattern of unfavorable child outcomes related to high levels of destructive IPC. These negative consequences may be long-lasting, at least into the college years for people across cultural contexts (Bradford et al., 2003). For example, Bradford et al. (2003) conducted a large-scale study of IPC, spillover, and adolescent outcomes in 11 countries on five continents. Several ethnic majority and minority cultures were represented in this study of over 9,000 teenagers who were 14–17 years old. They found that IPC is both directly and indirectly linked to negative outcomes of depression and antisocial behavior in adolescents.

For the direct link, they found that overt IPC (characterized by open disagreement with threats, yelling, insults, etc.) was associated with higher levels of adolescent depression and antisocial behavior in all 11 countries. They also found that covert IPC (characterized by triangulation, unverbalized tension, etc.) was associated with higher levels of adolescent depression and antisocial behavior in every country except Bangladesh.

Bradford et al. (2003) also found that IPC indirectly affects adolescent outcomes by affecting parenting quality (demonstrating the spillover effect). For instance, they found that IPC was associated with significantly less parental support and behavioral control but with significantly more parental psychological control. Thinking back to high-school years, the reader might easily relate to these parenting qualities. Parental support is characterized by behaviors such as cheering up the child, listening to problems, and such. Parental behavioral control is characterized by behaviors such as knowing where the teenager *actually* is (rather than where she/he is *supposed* to be), knowing how he/she spends money, etc. Parental support and behavioral control are positive. Parental psychological control, on the other hand, is viewed negatively and includes focusing on past mistakes, trying to change the child's mind about something, and such. In the Bradford et al. study, these three parenting qualities also represented links between IPC and different levels of adolescent depression, antisocial behavior, and social initiative. They concluded that "risk to adolescent functioning associated with the presence of overt IPC can be explained by way of decreased parenting quality that accompanies overt IPC" (Bradford et al., 2003, p. 129).

Tactical Differences

Although consistent and patterned links exist between destructive IPC and child outcomes, evidence also exists that cultural nuances to family conflict processes occur across cultures. For example, Feldman et al. (2010) conducted a rigorous study of parent–child, interparental, and peer conflict in Israeli and Palestinian families. Israelis represent a fairly individualistic culture that values autonomy, whereas Palestinians represent a fairly collectivistic culture that values relational embeddedness (Feldman et al., 2010; Shamir et al., 2005). Consistent with previous research, Feldman et al. (2010) found that "higher spousal undermining behavior, more marital hostility, and less authoritative parenting predicted greater child aggression in both cultures" (p. 321). These findings highlight both the direct and indirect links between IPC and child outcomes across cultures.

However, they also found cultural differences in ways that conflict was handled in participating families. Feldman et al. (2010) noted:

> . . . [a]mong Israeli families, the typical way of asking was by request, the most common reaction was to negotiate, and the most frequent resolution was compromise, and compromise was as frequent a resolution in conflicts initiated by the mother, father, or child . . . among Palestinian families, demand was a more frequent way of asking, consent and object – which provide immediate response and limit further negotiation – occurred nearly three quarters of the time, and consent was the typical resolution . . . Israeli couples displayed more emotional empathy, particularly mothers, and Palestinian couples showed more instrumental solutions, especially fathers. (pp. 322–3)

Israeli children who witnessed negotiation and compromise at home tended to use those tactics in their peer conflicts, whereas

Palestinian children who witnessed authoritative consent at home tended to turn to adults for help during peer conflicts. Results from this study indicate that negative aspects of IPC seem to generalize across cultural contexts but culturally specific ways families model conflict resolution exist that are functional for children to take into other contexts, such as with peer conflict.

Implications

How people manage conflict when married, divorced, or remarried impacts children and their future relationships. Many of the findings we presented might appear obvious, though the specific factors studied probably were unexpected.

First, we discussed several features of interparental conflict (IPC). These include spillover, triangulation, and appraisals. Let us consider spillover: the research shows that how married couples treat each other connects to how they treat their children. In other words, despite their wishes, parents often cannot isolate their problems or conflict behaviors from their children. One should not expect to – children are perceptive.

Second, the interparental conflict literature shows that conflict messages affect children's adjustment problems directly and indirectly. Conflict messages are first interpreted by the child in terms of the child's well-being. The appraisals of threat and blame are the two primary concerns. Then those appraisals and levels of emotional security directly affect children's internalizing and externalizing problems. Although you might expect that changes in conflict communication can lead to differential results (and they often will), one must also take care to validate the child, indicating the IPC is not about him/her, does not threaten to bring him/her into the middle of it, and does not threaten his/her security.

Third, divorce is now normative. The increased divorce rate coupled with increased acceptance of divorce as a smart option to relational dissatisfaction imply that more and more romantic relationships are unstable. Managing the unexpected here means understanding one's place in a culture that accepts divorce and, more specifically, understanding that the intergenerational transmission of divorce can affect your personal relationships. The marital status of women's parents is especially important (as it affects both women and men in heterosexual relationships). Conflicts regarding commitment, for example, could very well stem from one's attitudes toward divorce as well as the partner's parents' marital status.

Next, it is clear that stepfamilies vary quite a bit from intact families. And stepfamilies take different forms or types. However, these families (which can appear rather instantly) can be ill-formed because they are ill-thought. Recall that only about 40 percent of couples discuss how they would coparent the children (Cartwright, 2010). Ganong et al. (2006) argued that people put so little thought into stepfamilies because they are naïve ("it won't be that hard"), avoidant (they do not discuss the important topics of finances or parenting), lack resources (e.g., information about stepfamilies), and adopt myths about marriage and stepfamilies (e.g., having a traditional family is best for everyone). Likewise, Bray and Kelly (1998) emphasize how important it is to discuss parenting expectations and styles. Clearly, managing the unexpected here means communicating with one's partner about what would define the stepfamily and how to raise the children. Things simply won't work out because you believe they will. More likely than not, conflict will ensue and the parent of the child(ren) will want final say about parenting and discipline. Based on these discussions, one or both partners might have to recalibrate expectations about what stepfamily life will look like.

Fourth, negative impacts of destructive interparental communication seem to be universal. Contrary to the attenuation hypothesis, research has not revealed that certain ethnic minority groups are less vulnerable to harmful outcomes because they have extended family members to "make up" for bad parenting (Feldman et al., 2010) or because they are exposed to other stresses that "mute" the impact of IPC (Shamir et al., 2005). Rather, hostility in marriage, lack of parental support (for each other and for children), and lack of behavioral control over children (authoritative parenting) constitute direct and indirect links of IPC and harmful outcomes for children, such as depression, aggression, and anti-social behavior. On the other hand, there do seem to be culturally specific pathways for productive conflict management in families that then transfer to ways children handle conflicts outside of the family, such as at school. Accordingly, culture seems to make more of a difference for constructive interparental conflict management than it does for destructive interparental conflict.

Finally, conflict communication is implicated throughout the chapter. Perhaps unexpectedly, a combination of communication behaviors appears to affect children. The effects of communication can be direct, as when we see how negative, frequent, and unresolved conflict between parents can leave a child vulnerable. And the effects can be indirect. Aggressive communication and inappropriate disclosures about an absent parent can lead to the child's feeling caught in the middle, which then can lead to dissatisfaction with the parent and (again) adjustment problems. These invisible indirect effects that live between communication and consequences can be the most unexpected (and unwanted) guest in the home.

4

Conflict between Parents and Children

Twelve year-old Brad entered his mother's home office, where she was working on the computer, to let her know he was going to play basketball at the park with his friend, Jim.

Brad: *This is Jim's cell phone number.*

Mom: *He got a cell phone for Christmas?*

Brad: *Yeah. I need a cell phone. All of my friends have cell phones. I need to be able to call them when I'm riding around outside.*

Mom: *Need? How about want. You want a cell phone.*

Brad: *No, need. I get one this summer.*

Mom: *[silence, raising eyebrows]*

Brad: *Matt [his brother] got one before he went into 8th grade.*

Mom: *Matt got one for his 14th birthday, which just happened to be in the summer before 8th grade.*

Brad: *Exactly. So he got one before 8th grade, so I get one before 8th grade.*

Historically, researchers have invested a great deal of time studying parent–child (P-C) conflict. Both lay individuals and researchers regard particular child development stages as especially highly conflict laden – mostly those periods involving the "terrible twos" and adolescence. People's expectations that conflict increases during preschool years rose partly in the belief that parents could gain control over toddler misbehavior. Likewise, people sought explanations for why teenagers become disenchanted with previously sacred spaces and want to create their own uncertain messes, especially when these maturing children use behaviors that degrade parents and disrupt the entire family.

Parents and researchers (and even counselors) might have hoped to some degree (likely with different reasons) that once these hallmark phases of P-C conflict passed, members of the family would return home looking and behaving very much like they did when they were younger. But now we know that the unexpected often trumps the expected. The potholes and curves of family life are seldom mapped; and existing signposts offer only vague representations of how one should travel to the next destination. Just as surprisingly, the rearview mirror will likely reflect more interesting P-C relationships and (amazingly) some view of how P-C conflicts occur as a function of one's own development (Canary et al., 1995). In a word, parent–child conflict cannot be meaningfully segmented unless we obtain information about children and personal development, relational contexts, and the ever-important processes that create and recreate family relationships.

Naturally, P-C conflict should be more expected than unexpected, considering the assumed hierarchical nature of parent–child relationships and the enormous developmental changes that occur in children throughout their life (Adams & Laursen, 2001). Conflict interactions between parents and children reflect relational dynamics, developmental processes, and cultural expectations. Research indicates that P-C conflict influences, and is influenced by, other family experiences such as child behavior and parent–child relationship qualities (Burt et al., 2005; Ostrov & Bishop, 2008). Further, researchers have traced the impacts of P-C conflict over time, showing how conflict during one developmental stage affects behavior and relationship qualities at later stages, including partner relationships in young adulthood (Burt et al., 2005; Overbeek et al., 2007).

We hold that family conflict processes, and P-C conflict in particular, are best understood by expecting the unexpected. We use this chapter to highlight the main issues identified in research regarding topics, processes, and outcomes of P-C conflict. We first discuss P-C conflict in early childhood before moving to research on parent–adolescent conflict, conflict between parents and their adult children, and interesting issues that arise within particular cultural contexts. We conclude by highlighting implications for managing parent–child conflict.

Conflict between Parents and Young Children

Much of the research concerning conflict between parents and young children includes samples of children who are roughly between two and four years old. This developmental stage represents a time of increased linguistic and cognitive skills, essentially providing the communicative tools with which young children *can* engage in conflict with their parents. Conflict in the toddler years is quite frequent. Researchers often cite Dix's (1991) finding that parent–toddler conflicts occur on average between 3.5 and 15 times *an hour*(!). However, mother–toddler dyads in one recent study (Laible et al., 2008) averaged 20–25 conflicts per hour in laboratory and home contexts, with tremendous variability in frequency from 4–55 conflicts per hour. As indicated in chapter 1, these conflicts are measured at the linguistic level (for example, as two opposing statements) that tend to reflect benign issues (Canary et al., 1995). That is, a "conflict" is said to occur when one person opposes another person's position. Eisenberg (1992), for example, reported nine conflicts per hour with toddlers. She noted, however, that these conflicts were very brief (i.e., not elaborated) and yielded minimal relational fallout. Although such behaviors might constitute conflict in a social linguistic sense, their length and severity are likely less alarming than an initial read might imply.

According to Caughy et al. (2009), P-C conflict peaks when children are between two and three years old and decreases after children are four years old. Even research with very young children (16–18 months old) has identified important patterns in P-C conflict (Huang et al., 2007). Less research focuses on children in the early elementary years (5–8 years old).

Conflict Topics

When considering conflicts with young children, many people think of the numerous "No!"s that toddlers proclaim or the many times young children shout "Mine!" about possessions. However, research reveals an interesting range of conflict topics emerging between parents (mostly mothers) and their young children.

One such topic concerns rules – socially or family based (Huang et al., 2007; Laible & Thompson, 2002; Laible et al., 2008). Conflicts about these issues can be recognized by parents correcting, reprimanding, or otherwise responding to children violating a rule, such as eating sweets before dinner, reaching for a prohibited item, and creating a mess. Rule violations are fairly predictable for toddlers who can readily comply physically.

Such rule violations become more interesting and unexpected when these same toddlers realize they have the ability (1) to understand their own limitations, and (2) to tie those limits to the word "no." As toddlers explore their expanding universe, much that intrigues them will remain off-limits and parents will repeatedly teach those limits to young children. In one interesting study about food consumption involving 1–11-year-old children, Paugh and Izquierdo (2009) found that family conflict about food represents a battle of wills in the ways family rules are negotiated. As might be anticipated, what the parents want their children to eat often does not correspond to what the child wants. So the rules regarding who has the final say become quite important.

Importantly, rule violation and negotiation do not exhaust the only sources of P-C conflict in the early years. Table 4.1 lists common conflict topics that researchers have identified. Most parents will concur that frequent sources of conflict with young children include destructive and/or aggressive behavior, such as hitting, throwing things, and making a mess. Destruction more likely emerges when children have highly active temperaments but insecure attachment styles (Laible et al., 2008). That is, the child breaks things and does so without believing that she can or will receive support from the primary caregiver (in most cases, the mother). Laible et al. also found that mother–toddler dyads with

Table 4.1 Parent–Child Conflict in Early Childhood

Common Conflict Topics
- Destructive/aggressive behavior
- Physical space
- Manners/politeness
- Caretaking
- Possessions/rights/turns
- Rules
- Independence
- Facts

Common Conflict Processes
- Compromise
- Bargaining
- Justification
- Clarification
- Reasoning
- Threatening
- Teasing
- Simple insistence

Commonly Associated Positive Outcomes
- Emotional understanding
- Moral understanding
- Prosocial behavior
- Compliance

Commonly Associated Negative Outcomes
- Negative affect
- Oppositional responses
- Aversive/aggressive responses
- Relational aggression with others

secure attachment styles were more likely to argue about posses-sions, independence, and physical space than were insecure dyads. We see these conflict topics emerging among older cohorts, which we discuss later in this chapter.

Conflict Processes and Outcomes

Beyond the inherent interest factors of different topics, a critical concern involves how parents and children manage these conflicts in process and how conflict processes relate to other important aspects of child and family life. As table 4.1 suggests, high frequency of P-C conflict is not *necessarily* detrimental to P-C relationship quality or child development (Caughy et al., 2009). However, Ostrov and Bishop (2008) found that P-C conflict in preschoolers was positively associated with relational aggression at school. More importantly, researchers have identified that the *way* in which these conflicts emerge and continue associates in different ways with both consequences and outcomes. As the reader might expect, most of this research involves observations of mother–child dyads, so conclusions about parent–child conflict typically represent conclusions about mother–child conflict. However, Socha and Yingling (2010) provide an interesting scenario and discussion of conflict between a young boy and his father that allows us to imagine how findings from mother–child studies applies to father–child dyads. We provide an excerpt from their case here:

> A father and four-year-old son are just completing a grocery store purchase when, without dad noticing, his son grabs a candy bar from the display, opens it, and begins to eat it as he follows behind his dad toward the door . . . Before they reach the door, the clerk yells, "Hey! Your kid took a candy bar!" (Socha & Yingling, 2010, pp. 118–19)

The authors lead readers through an extended discussion of potential responses by the father, the son, and within the broader family. Their elaboration reflects research of constructive P-C conflict processes we discuss below.

Several constructive processes emerge in observations of mother–child conflict. For example, Laible and Thompson (2002) found that mothers' use of conflict mitigating strategies, such as compromise and bargaining, and justification strategies, such as clarifications and reasoning, were associated with several positive characteristics of 2½-year-olds six months later. These positive characteristic outcomes included chidlren's emotional under-standing, sociomoral competence, and prosocial perceptions of relationships. Similarly, Huang et al. (2007) found mothers' pref-erence for constructive responses, such as distraction, reasoning, or negotiation, and simple oppositional responses, such as saying "no," positively associated with children's adaptive responses (e.g., obeying or negotiating) but were negatively tied to overt oppositional responses (e.g., saying "no", throwing temper tan-trums). Consider the following example (from Eisenberg, 1992, p. 29), where the mother persuades the child through reasoning:

Speaker	Message
Child:	[Approaching sister's daycare] I'm gonna stay in the car.
Mother:	Why don't you come in and hold my hand, okay?
Child:	Uh-uh [meaning no]
Mother:	There's no reason to wait out in the car.
Child:	[Whines] Well, I want to. So let me, okay?
Mother:	Well, if you want to. Well, what about Tom and Emily? They're gonna wonder why you didn't come in. Do you wanna come and stand outside with them while I get Janie?
Child:	Yeah.

Interestingly, Laible and Thompson (2002) found that maternal references to rules and consequences during P-C conflict were not associated with socioemotional development in children. Consider the following example (from Dunn & Munn, 1985, p. 491), where the rule "it isn't nice" has little currency with the child:

Speaker	Message
Mother:	Don't pull my hair! Madam! Don't pull my hair. No. It's not nice to pull hair, is it?
Child:	Hair.
Mother:	Hair, yes, but you mustn't pull it, must you?
Child:	Yes! [smiles]
Mother:	No! No!
Child:	No!
Mother:	No. No. It's not kind to pull hair, is it?

Child: Nice!
Mother: No, it isn't.
Child: Nice!

Predictably, destructive conflict processes are associated with less positive outcomes for individuals and families. For instance, Huang et al. (2007) found destructive maternal responses, such as criticism and threatening, in P-C conflict interactions associated with unresolved conflicts. Paugh and Iazuierdo (2009) concluded that family conflicts regarding food and eating build over time and that parents in their study demonstrated uneasiness with authority and control as they engagd in battles of wills with their children. Ultimately, these families lacked positive interactions about food and eating choices that would relate food with pleasure, tastes, and positive affect. Forget dessert.

Conflict between Parents and Adolescents

Intergenerational conflict increases in intensity as children get closer to young adulthood (Smetana et al., 2003). Although the number of conflicts between parents and their adolescent children might not increase from the 20–25 linguistic events per hour seen between parents and toddlers, adolescence represents a highly conflictual phase of development between teens and their parents (e.g., Adams & Laursen, 2001; Allison & Schultz, 2004; Smetana et al., 2003). Adolescents spend less time with their parents than do younger children, which along with increased P-C conflict is part of the natural developmental process of individuation (Adams & Laursen, 2001; Dotterer et al., 2008). In terms of a broad picture, P-C conflict frequency tends to be lower in early and late adolescence but peak in mid-adolescence (Smetana et al., 2003). This inverted U pattern reflects developmental processes of children learning to establish their identities in a conflictual manner and then finding their way into adulthood with less conflict.

    Because adolescents develop their own identities as they differentiate themselves from the family, the nature of the parent–child relationship involves high levels of conflict. Parents and teens typically still live in the same household that contain rules that parents typically established without the collaboration of their teenage children (Adams & Laursen, 2001). Thus, a tug of war exists between a family system that involves obligatory relationships, unilateral rules, and compulsory interactions against a developmental adolescent stage that involves self-determination, individuation, and a desire to differentiate from parents (Adams & Laursen, 2001). One side pulls at how things used to be; the other side pulls at how things will be.

Smetana's (1988, 1989) research illustrates this tug of war. She discovered that adolescents and parents both know what the other is thinking with regard to *personal issues*. These issues include getting piercings, keeping one's room clean, sleeping in, choosing friends, and other behaviors that reflect one's personal control of one's life. However, the parent and the adolescent disagree that the other person even has a right to enforce his/her opinions regarding personal matters, so conflict ensues.

Such boundaries that distinguish childhood from adulthood spring up quite unexpectedly. From our own experience with our sons and stepsons, we have seen how daily hassles find their way into frequent interactions during their adolescent years. When our boys were early adolescents, it was a simple matter of reminding them of their responsibilities before they could enjoy privileges such as going to movies with their friends. These reminders often led to negotiations or conflicts about expectations. As they got older, however, daily hassles about keeping their rooms clean and participating in general household chores took on an added dimension of their desire for autonomy and to be treated like young adults rather than children. This is likely one reason this topic emerges across age cohorts.

As mentioned above, adolescence is a time for individuation. In that process, teens want to be more self-directed than parent-directed. Reminders and requirements about taking care of their spaces, their possessions, and maintaining their responsibilities to the larger family unit impinge on those ideas of being self-directed. As Heather once reminded her 18-year-old son, "You are not an island. What you do affects us all." His blank stare indicated that he had never reflected on this idea before!

Conflict Topics

Several researchers have investigated conflict topics that emerge as most important or frequent in parent–adolescent relationships. Table 4.2 lists common conflict topics for parent–adolescent dyads as well as conflict processes and outcomes identified in research. One common topic across adolescent age groups is daily hassles, such as care of room, household chores, and homework. These topics emerge as frequent sources of conflict in early adolescence (Allison & Schultz, 2004), mid-adolescence (Barber & Delfabbro, 2000), and late adolescence (Adams & Laursen, 2001).

Table 4.2   Parent–Child Conflict in Adolescence

Common Conflict Topics
- Household chores
- Room care
- Homework/school performance
- Autonomy
- Relationships
- Personal appearance

Common Conflict Processes
- Demand/withdraw
- Problem solving
- Compromise
- Coercion

Commonly Associated Positive Outcomes
- Individuation
- Identity development
- Higher academic achievement

Commonly Associated Negative Outcomes
- Externalizing behavioral problems
- Internalizing behavioral problems
- Lower academic achievement

The connection between daily hassles and individuation leads to another frequent conflict topic in adolescence – autonomy. Allison and Schultz (2004) found that autonomy was one of the least frequent conflict topics in their study of sixth–eighth graders, but Adams and Laursen (2001) found it to be a frequent topic in their study of teens ranging from 15 to 18 years old. This difference between age cohorts makes sense when considering activities that differ between junior high and high school. Teens in junior high school cannot drive nor do they have jobs. Accordingly, they still depend on their parents, to a large degree, for financial support and for transportation to their various activities. However, as teens hit the 16-year-old mark, they are typically eligible in the US to drive and they can work longer hours for pay outside the home. These opportunities naturally foster a sense of autonomy, self-direction, and independence.

Findings regarding P-C conflict about *relationships* do not coincide across age cohorts, though they can remain a source of conflict. For example, Allison and Schultz (2004) included an item about choosing friends. Overall, this was not viewed by many participants as an important area of P-C conflict. However, in both the Adams and Laursen (2001) study and the Barber and Delfabbro (2000) study, relationships/friends emerged as a frequent source of conflict between parents and older (high school) adolescents. Importantly, Barber and Delfabbro found that parents' relationships with their teenagers' friends connected to adolescent adjustment as well as the sheer amount of daily hassles fathers gave their adolescent sons. This finding indicates that adolescents' peer relationships, and their parents' relationships with their peers, can increase parent–adolescent conflict even when it is not specifically identified as a conflict topic.

Conflict Processes and Outcomes

Although knowing what topics serve as sources of conflict between parents and adolescents can transform the unexpected into the expected, perhaps a more interesting line of inquiry concerns how conflicts unfold between parents and teens, including outcomes related to different conflict processes. Many studies have found a general trend where conflicts increase from early to mid-adolescence and then decrease as children move into late adolescence (e.g., Allison & Schultz, 2004; Smetana et al., 2003). Smetana et al. (2003) considered pre-teens and early adolescents to include children between 10 and 12 years old and middle adolescents to include children between 13 and 16 years old. We can conclude that late adolescence includes children from 17 to 19 years old, although other researchers consider college students 18 years old and older as "adults." It is pretty clear that not only is adolescence a difficult stage in life; it is also difficult to agree on how to categorize age cohorts.

Although conflict frequency follows a curvilinear path as teens mature, research has also found that conflict intensity steadily increases throughout adolescence (Cicognani & Zani, 2010; Flannery et al., 1993; Smetana et al., 2003). Accordingly, we cannot make sweeping generalizations about the adolescent stage without taking into account different phases of development during the stage. A 12-year-old clearly differs from a 17-year-old. Most researchers recognize this and clearly state their results as relating to early, middle, or late adolescence. Accordingly, we discuss P-C conflict processes and outcomes in these three developmental phases.

Early adolescence

Because adolescence promotes individuation, teens and parents are likely (even more likely than the rest of us) to have different perceptions of the same experiences. Sillars et al. (2010) recognized this possibility and studied parents' and adolescents' perceptions after parent–child conflict. Participating teens were in sixth–eighth grade, so they were early–mid adolescents. Their findings support the idea that teens and parents interpret interactions differently. For example, parents in their study over-attributed negative thoughts to their adolescents, whereas adolescents over-attributed controlling thoughts to their parents (Sillars et al., 2010, p. 742). The researchers noted that these differing perceptions could lead to inadvertent escalation of conflict.

Importantly, parent–adolescent dyads are not isolated from other family members. As introduced in chapter 1, families can be seen as systems. Parent–child relationships thus represent subsystems that are influenced by, and influence, other subsystems in the family. Due to the interrelatedness of family subsystems, researchers have examined how parent–child conflict functions in relation to other subsystems, such as the parental dyad (e.g., El-Sheikh & Elmore-Staton, 2004; Rinaldi & Howe, 2003; van Doorn et al., 2007; chapter 3). A number of outcomes related to parental dyadic conflict were discussed in chapter 3, but we have the opportunity here to review findings regarding associations between marital conflict and parent–child conflict, particularly in the pre-teen and early adolescent years.

Researchers consistently find connections between ways in which couples engage in conflict and ways in which they engage in conflict with their adolescent children. Findings have been interpreted with different systems-based perspectives, such as the emotional security framework (Cummings & Davies, 2010; El-Sheikh & Elmore-Staton, 2004), the family spillover hypothesis (Rinaldi & Howe, 2003), and the transmission model (van Doorn et al., 2007). For example, Rinaldi and Howe (2003) examined associations between dimensions of marital conflict, sibling conflict, and parent–child conflict. Children recruited for their study were early adolescents in fifth and sixth grades, with an average age of 11.5 years. Results of that study indicate that parent–child reasoning, verbal aggression, and avoidance conflict strategies were positively correlated with the same strategies in marital conflict (Rinaldi & Howe, 2003, p. 455). These researchers reasoned that results confirm the spillover hypothesis that what occurs in one family subsystem has a spillover effect on other family subsystems. We will discuss findings regarding associations with sibling conflict in chapter 5. As referenced earlier, Van Doorn et al. (2007) conducted a two-year longitudinal study of conflict across family subsystems to determine whether an explanation other than the spillover hypothesis might be used to understand how subsystems influence family members over time. Participants in the van Doorn et al. study were in the young–middle adolescent years at Time 1 (*M* = 13.2 years old). Although the researchers acknowledged that the spillover hypothesis might be at play, at least partially, they used independent reports of marital and P-C conflict at two points in time to also be able to identify one-way influence. As mentioned, van Doorn et al. (2007) found that parents' use of positive problem solving and negative conflict engagement, but not withdrawal, positively associated with adolescents' use of the same strategies in parent–child conflict two years later. However, bi-directionality of influence was not found, indicating that there is a stronger influence in conflict dynamics from parents to children than the other way around. According to the researchers, these results support a *transmission* model of family interaction behavior in that adolescents are more likely to learn from and model behavior from parents than parents are from their children.

When determining outcomes of family conflict dynamics, results are a bit more complex. For instance, El-Sheikh and Elmore-Staton (2004) tested mediating and moderating models for marital conflict, P-C conflict, and behavior problems in elementary schoolchildren and young adolescents. Again, a *mediating* model examines how one variable connects the effects of one variable on a third variable; a *moderating* model examines how one variable changes the levels of effects of one variable on a third variable. Results from that study indicate that mother–child conflict fully connected the effects of externalizing problems for younger children, meaning that parental conflict and elementary school-aged children's externalizing problems were linked *through* mother–child conflict. However, mother–child conflict only explained some of the internalizing effects of marital conflict. Likewise, father–child conflict only partially explained the connection between marital conflict and externalizing problems (El-Sheikh & Elmore-Staton, 2004, p. 642). In a moderating manner, mother–child and father–child conflict influenced the association between marital conflict and child behavior problems. When examining this effect, results indicate that "higher levels of externalizing problems were predicted for children with higher levels of mother–child conflict regardless of marital conflict" (El-Sheikh & Elmore-Staton, 2004, p. 638).

A similar effect was found for father–child conflict, but higher father–child conflict magnified marital conflict effects on externalizing problems. Father–child conflict also was a moderator for the connection between marital conflict and internalizing problems for boys, but not girls. In sum, results of this study indicate that parent–child conflict plays an important role in child behavioral outcomes in the context of marital conflict, but these roles are complex and not as simple as one might expect.

Some people might wonder if these child outcomes, such as externalizing behavior (i.e., acting out) and internalizing behavior (i.e., depressive symptoms), are more tied to child-specific characteristics than to parent–child interaction dynamics. Burt et al. (2006) designed a study with identical twins to answer this question. Not only did they study adolescents who were genetically the same, they studied parent–child conflict and outcomes over time in a longitudinal design that measured P-C conflict and child behavior when the children were 11, 14, and 17 years old. They found that when twins had markedly different levels of either externalizing behaviors or P-C conflict, the twin who engaged in more parent–child conflict at 11 years old also engaged in more externalizing behaviors at 14 years old. These results indicate that one should not expect children from the same family to grow up the same. Even identical twins can have different conflict behaviors early in adolescence that affect them years later.

Middle adolescence

Parent–child conflict in early and middle adolescents affects behavioral outcomes in teens. Furthermore, we know from the research discussed in the previous section that ways in which parents solve their own conflicts influence how parent–child conflicts are handled. Research with participants in middle adolescence sheds more light on these issues by examining different conflict strategies and tactics used in parent–adolescent conflict and outcomes related to various conflict message processes.

Several studies reveal common strategies used in parent–adolescent conflicts. For example, Adams and Laursen (2001) compared conflict dynamics in parent–child dyads and friend dyads. Their mid-adolescent participants indicated that conflicts with their parents were characterized by more angry affect than conflicts with their friends. Also, resolutions with parents were obtained mostly by deferring to demands, and more win–lose outcomes occccurred with parents than conflicts with their friends. These results corroborate previous findings that negative affect increases and positive affect decreases as adolescents mature (Flannery et al., 1993). Because parent–child conflicts also involved more daily hassles than did friend conflicts, it is easy to see how P-C conflicts appear much more severe, anger-laden, and compliant to the parent's wishes (Flannery et al., 1993).

Moreover, these characteristics of parent–adolescent conflict (intensity, anger, compliance) could also lead to adolescent withdrawal from conflict. Although the demand–withdraw pattern is most commonly associated with romantic couple conflict, Caughlin and Malis (2004) reasoned that the pattern probably exists in parent–adolescent dyads as well. Accordingly, they examined patterns of parent–demand/adolescent–withdraw and how this pattern associates with relationship satisfaction. As might be expected, these researchers found that parents' and middle adolescents' reports of relational satisfaction negatively correlated with the parent–demand/adolescent–withdraw conflict pattern. That is, the more participants reported the demand–withdraw pattern in their P-C conflicts, the less they reported being satisfied with their parent–child relationships. One can envision a parent who wants compliance to be making demands and criticizing the adolescent, whose primary goal is simply to get out of the conflict.

In addition to relational satisfaction, research links parent–adolescent conflict interaction patterns with other relationship outcomes. For example, Cicognani and Zani (2010) recruited 13- and 15-year-olds and their families to report on their conflict strategies and outcomes. Participants in their study reported using compromise strategies more than aggressive strategies and their conflicts tended to end with more intimacy than frustration. These results are promising in light of the more negative perceptions of conflict interactions reported by Adams and Laursen (2001).

Other researchers have been interested in links between parent–adolescent conflict interactions and outcomes such as school performance, delinquency, and other behavioral problems (Adams & Laursen, 2007; Branje et al., 2009; Dotterer et al., 2008). Adams and Laursen (2007) examined links between P-C conflict frequencies, P-C relationship quality (in terms of levels of negativity in the relationship), and adolescent outcomes of delinquency (a type of externalizing behavior), school grades, and withdrawal (a type of internalizing behavior). Their findings shed light on the complexities of P-C conflict.

For instance, increased conflict from low to medium levels was related to higher school grades for adolescents in better quality P-C relationships (in terms of lower levels of negativity). However, the same low to medium increase in conflict levels was related to higher levels of delinquency and withdrawal for adolescents in poorer quality P-C relationships (in terms of higher levels of negativity). Importantly, high levels of P-C conflict were never related to positive outcomes, such as higher school grades. These results complement those found by Dotterer et al. in their study of P-C conflict and school grades. Dotterer et al. (2008) found a bi-directional association between parent–adolescent conflict and grades over a two-year time period. Specifically, they found a significant relationship between higher levels of mother–adolescent and father–adolescent conflict when participants were an average of 15 years old and participants' English and math grades two years later. At the same time, there was a similar significant association between lower English and math grades at Time 1 and higher levels of conflict with both parents two years later.

These studies indicate that more than simple frequency counts should be taken into consideration when examining parent–child conflict dynamics and outcomes over time. Branje et al. (2009) worked from this assumption in their study of adolescent age, conflict resolution styles, and adjustment outcomes. Their study also sheds light on potential positive outcomes of parent–adolescent conflict. For example, Branje et al. found that older adolescents (mean age of 16.7 years old) were more likely than younger adolescents (mean age of 12.4 years old) to use positive conflict resolution styles, such as trying to understand the other person, using reasoning, and searching for compromise. On the other hand, younger adolescents were more likely than older adolescents to use negative resolution styles, such as attacking the other, being verbally abusive, or withdrawing. Younger adolescents also were more likely than older adolescents to employ a "no resolution" style that involves "ending all contact without resolving the conflict" (Branje et al., 2009, p. 197). As one might anticipate, these behaviors among early adolescents led to more externalizing problems (i.e., delinquency) when they used withdrawal to resolve conflicts with their parents, and more internalizing problems (i.e., anxiety or depression) when they combined negative conflict resolution styles, including aggression, withdrawal, and exit ("no resolution"). On a positive note, adolescents who used effective conflict resolution strategies, characterized by high levels of positive problem solving and low levels of the negative styles of aggression, withdrawal, and exit, reported only low to medium levels of conflict with their parents and also had lower levels of externalizing and internalizing adjustment problems.

From these studies of parent–adolescent conflict processes and outcomes we can conclude that conflict dynamics between parents and their adolescent children clearly intertwine with other aspects of family dynamics and family members. At the same time, parent–adolescent conflict interactions have implications for important academic and social outcomes. Differences in both processes and outcomes for younger and older adolescents point to the developmental changes that occur within this stage of family life. They also reveal areas for intervention to teach positive conflict management behaviors to adolescents and their parents. We can see from research that parent–adolescent conflict does *not have* to be detrimental. Indeed, researchers have found that low to medium levels of conflict, when managed constructively within positive parent–child relationships, can be beneficial to children and to the family system as a whole.

Table 4.3 Parent–Child Conflict in Adulthood

Common Conflict Topics
- Communication and interaction style
- Habits and lifestyle choices
- Child-rearing practices and values
- Politics
- Religion and ideology
- Work habits
- Household maintenance

Common Conflict Processes
- Avoidance
- Verbal aggression

Commonly Associated Positive Outcomes
- Higher relationship quality

Commonly Associated Negative Outcomes
- Lower relationship quality

Conflict between Parents and Adult Children

Considerably less research exists on conflict between parents and their adult children. We view this research area as a rich opportunity for future research. Societies across the globe are experiencing aging populations, and the trend is expected to continue (United Nations, 2012). For example, in the United States people 65 years and older represented about 12 percent of the national population but they are expected to constitute about 19 percent of the population by 2030 (US Administration on Aging, 2011). Although we do not know as much from empirical studies of parent–adult child conflict, we discuss common conflict topics, processes, and outcomes in this section, with strong encouragement for communication researchers to pursue this line of research. Table 4.3 summarizes this information.

Conflict Topics

As with studies involving adolescents and their parents, adult children and their parents have different perceptions of sources of their conflicts with each other. Clarke et al. (1999) conducted a qualitative study about inter-generational relationships and found six sources of conflict most commonly identified by older parents and their adult children. Parent participants in their study had an average age of 62 years and children participants in their study had an average age of 39 years. The six common conflict topics were: (1) communication and interaction style; (2) habits and lifestyle choices; (3) child-rearing practices and values; (4) politics, religion, and ideology; (5) work habits and orientations; and (6) household standards or maintenance (Clarke et al., p. 261). Parents most frequently identified conflicts over habits and lifestyle choices, whereas adult children most frequently identified communication and interaction style as the source of conflicts with their parents. These differences might be further understood by reviewing what we know about processes in these parent–child conflicts.

Conflict Processes and Outcomes

Research regarding conflict processes in this later family stage coincides with research about conflict processes and outcomes in earlier stages. For example, Birditt et al. (2009) found that "constructive strategies predicted greater relationship quality, whereas destructive and avoidant strategies predicted lower relationship quality" (p. 775). Adult children in their study, 22–49 years old, and parents, 40–84 years old, completed self-reports about ways in which they were most likely to handle tensions with their parent/child and also rated their perceptions about the relationship in terms of affective solidarity (positive relationship quality) and ambivalence (negative relationship quality). Results of this study indicate that parent–child relationships continue to be dynamic into later stages of the family life cycle and conflict management processes constitute an important part of how those relationships are maintained.

Perceptions of parent–adult child conflict processes also associated with individual characteristics. For example, Avtgis (2002) studied the role of internal (vs. external) locus of control in adult children's perceptions of conflicts with their parents. An internal (vs. external) locus of control concerns the extent to which you believe that your successes and failures are due to your own abilities and efforts, and not due to luck or other people (Canary & Lakey (with Marmo), 2013). Avtgis found that adult children with internal locus of control orientations reported feeling less persecuted in P-C conflicts than did participants with moderate or external locus of control orientations. Furthermore, this study revealed that participants with internal control orientations also reported less stress reactions to conflict than the other two groups as well as greater positive and less negative relational effects from P-C conflict than the other two groups. Relatedly, Copstead et al. (2001) reported that those with internal control orientations had higher tendencies to engage in conflict with their parents, although participants who had external control orientations reported using more verbal aggressiveness toward their parents. On the whole, these related studies highlight the importance of taking individual traits into consideration when looking at process and outcomes of parent–child conflict across the lifespan.

Single-Parent Families and Conflict

At this point, we discuss conflict in single-parent families. Given the recent explosion of adults who are raising children on their own (see below), a section devoted to this type of family is warranted. By "single-parent," we refer to homes in which only one adult raises the child(ren). This could refer to a divorced but never remarried individual or to someone who was never married but is a parent. We first offer a few observations regarding single-parent families; then we discuss conflict in single-parent families.

Observations on Single-Parent Families

First, the majority of single-parents are women, and approximately 40 percent of children born as of 2007 were to unmarried women (Socha & Yingling, 2010). Socha and Yingling also emphasize how never-married fathers as well as divorced fathers exit the scene, and less than half remain in contact with the child. Moreover, much of that contact might be quite negative or toxic. As Socha and Yingling stated, "Having a toxic relationship with father, or one that decreased in closeness, is more harmful than no relationship at all" (2010, p. 52). However, having a devoted single father tends to be as effective as having a devoted single mother, at least in terms of child outcomes such as academic achievement (Dufur et al., 2010).

Second, single parents endure challenges due to work–life conflicts. We elaborate on "work–life" conflict in the final chapter. Here, we refer to the research that documents how single parents, more that dual parents, must somehow negotiate demands at work with demands at home. Laursen (2005), for instance, noted that single mothers more likely work full-time but enjoy fewer social and economic resources than do married mothers. Laursen stated that these fewer resources increase stress, which in turn leads to family conflict. Likewise, Hilton and Desrochers (2000) found that greater economic strain on single mothers affected their role coping and parental control which, in turn, increased children's disruptive behavior.

Next, the daily routines and awareness of the child's whereabouts reflect the strain on single parents. Work demands on mothers decrease the experience of routines at home that are important to child adjustment (McLoyd et al., 2008). Hetheringon (1989) found that single mothers monitored their children less. Also, they knew less of where they were and what they were doing. And children of single mothers have less adult supervision when the parent is absent (Hetherington, 1989).

Fourth, depression tends to occur in greater frequency with single parents. Kurdek (1991) found that single-parent mothers were more depressed than women in low-conflict marriages (but not women in high-conflict marriages). McLoyd and colleagues (2008) found that work–family conflict lead to depression in single parents (which was linked to lack of routines in the home and child adjustment problems). And Dorsey et al. (2007) found that depression was an indicator of maternal distress; maternal distress negatively associated with positive parenting (e.g., consistency in parenting).

Fifth, children in single-parent homes tend to be less well-adjusted than are children in two-parent homes. For example, Kurdek (1991) found that negative behaviors of children (an externalization adjustment factor) occurred more in divorced and single-parent homes than in two-parent homes. However, Houser et al. (1993) reported that how conflict is managed in the home affects child adjustment more than does family status (single-parent vs. two-parent homes).

Finally, one might hope that other family members (or friends or neighbors) would step in to help. However, these "coparenting" relationships can generate conflicts of their own. Dorsey et al. (2007) found that single-mother conflict with co-caregivers positively associated with the mothers' distress, which was tied to negative parenting behavior through a spillover effect. Hetherington (1989) found that single mothers would prefer to be independent of their parents' support, if they could simply afford to do so.

Conflict in Single-Parent Families

Issues at conflict in single-parent homes appear to resemble the kinds of issues we discussed earlier. Smetana et al. (1991) reported these top seven conflict issues for their early- to mid-adolescent sample: (1) chores; (2) activities (parent regulation of); (3) interpersonal relationships; (4) homework/achievement; (5) bedtime curfew; (6) appearance; and (7) friendships (parent regulation of). As you can see, many of these topics reflect on the individuation process that adolescents must accomplish, regardless of whether they are in single- or two-parent homes. The big difference between the two homes concerns how single mothers "are typically the lone adult agent of socialization in the home, so to them fall all conflicts arising from this responsibility" (Smetana et al., 1991, p. 64).

In terms of the amount of conflict, it appears that single-parent homes have more of it (Laursen, 2005). Laursen found that adolescents expressed more frequent and more angry disagreements with single mothers compared to adolescents in two-parent homes. An examination of dinner conversations involving children 7–9 years old showed that single mothers fight more with their sons than do single fathers or married parents. However, Smetana et al. (1991) found that adolescents in single-parent homes viewed their conflict as less serious than did adolescents in married homes.

Some research suggests that greater antagonism occurs when conflict emerges in single-parent families. Capaldi et al. (1994) compared single-parent to two-parent families in terms of the nonverbal messages sent during conflict. These authors found that single mothers showed more contempt and fewer neutral nonverbal messages toward their early adolescent sons than did married mothers. In a study of child sex differences, Brach et al. (2000) found that single mothers fought more with sons than daughters, whereas in two-parent homes mothers fought more with daughters. Also, daughters were more active in conflicts, which coincides with Laursen's (2005) research that girls report more conflict than do boys. Brach et al. (2000) concluded that the sex differences in conflict between the types of homes reflects "an underlying hostility towards the male child in many homes" (p. 88). Also, children in single-parent homes also appear to interrupt more than do children in married homes (Hetherington, 1989).

As we indicated in chapters 1, 2, and 3, different forms of families, marriages, and stepfamilies exist. The same principle holds for single-parent families. Using data that included a variety of factors, Hetherington (1989) reported three different clusters of children in single-parent homes. These indicate variations in the single-parent–child relationship and conflicts.

The first type of child is the *aggressive-insecure* child. This child is more non-compliant, has fewer friends, and suffers from adjustment problems. Step-families and single-parent families more likely contain this child. High levels of conflict, negative emotional responses, and poor conflict management skills typify this child.

The second child is the *opportunistic-competent*, who has high self-esteem, lots of friends, and good adjustment. What typifies this child concerns an ability to manipulate other people. The opportunistic-competent child ingratiates to people with power and can play adults off each other.

Finally, the *opportunistic-caring* child is well adjusted, has friends, assumes responsibility, but is not manipulative. Almost all opportunistic-caring children are girls and no boys from stepfamilies or single-parent homes were in this group. However, over 50 percent of the girls in this group are from single-parent homes or stepfamilies.

Cultural Considerations

One aspect of parent–child conflict that has garnered increased empirical attention concerns the role of culture in conflict interactions. More than mere demographics, culture pervades ways family members view their world, their roles, and their expectations of others (figure 1.3). It makes sense, then, that we consider cultural influences on parent–child conflict. Table 4.4 summarizes conflict topics, processes, and outcomes identified in research that focuses on cultural considerations.

Conflict Topics

Because families have become increasingly mobile, more opportunities exist for family members to experience different cultural contexts as they "do family." When families move from one country to another country with different cultural assumptions and practices, such as from Vietnam to Canada, children grow up with very different cultural experiences than their parents did. Several scholars have examined this difference and label the resulting phenomenon *acculturative family distancing* (Hwang, 2006), *cultural adaptation conflict* (Ahn et al., 2009), *acculturation gap*

Table 4.4 Parent–Child Conflict in Specific Cultural Contexts

Focal Culture	Common Topics	Common Processes	Associated Outcomes
Latino/Hispanic			• Internalizing behaviors • Externalizing behaviors
Asian	• Demands conflict with desire • Unreasonable behavior • Demands exceed ability • Role conflict • Interparental dispute • Immoral demands • Dating and marriage • Career/education • Family expectations		• Emotional distance • Interpersonal problems • Low self-confidence • Anxiety • Depression
African-American	• Chores • Cleaning room • Activities • TV, telephone, music • Homework/academic achievement • Interpersonal relations • Bedtime • Finances/spending	• Compromise • Punishment • Reasoning • Joint resolution • Parent unilateral resolution	

(Tsai-Chae & Nagata, 2008), or *intergenerational cultural disso-nance* (Choi et al., 2008). Regardless of the particular label, these terms all indicate that families moving across cultures face chal-lenges that mono-cultural families do not experience, and these challenges are a source of parent–child conflict. Indeed, Ahn et al. (2009) argue that family conflicts in these families may be largely explained by cultural differences between parents and children.

Children frequently adapt, or acculturate, to an adopted culture faster or more completely than parents and grandparents, leading to differences in value orientations, perspectives on family roles, and life goals across generations. For example, Ahn et al. (2009) and Tsai-Chae and Nagata (2008) noted that immigrant fami-lies, particularly those moving from Asian countries to western countries, commonly have conflicts about educational and career choices, family expectations, and dating and marriage.

However, immigrant families are not the only families expe-riencing cultural differences. Yeh and Bedford (2004) surveyed adolescents (13–19 years old) in Taiwan to investigate asso-ciations between P-C conflict frequency, conflict topics, and different types of filial beliefs (responsibility of children toward their elders). Adolescents in that study identified several sources of conflicts with their parents, including parent demands running counter to child desires, parents exhibiting unreasonable behavior, parent demands exceeding child ability, role conflict, interparen-tal disputes, and perceived immoral demands by parents. Results indicate that adolescents with absolute filial beliefs (those who adopt both authoritarian views of responsibilities and reciprocal views of responsibility to family members) have less P-C conflict than those adolescents with no filial beliefs. Because this study was conducted in Taiwan rather than in a Western nation, we might conclude that features of other cultures, such as American notions of low power-distance, affect family communication pro-cesses even in mono-cultural families. As adolescents use different cultural lenses to develop their value priorities, they tend to find themselves clashing with parents who cling to traditional cultural values and practices.

Because studies of families in the United States predominantly include participants who are white and middle class, Smetana et al. (2003) investigated whether P-C conflict topics identified in predominantly white samples apply to a sample of African American families. Fairly consistent with other studies of adolescent–parent conflict, participants identified the following topics most frequently: chores, cleaning room, choice of activities, TV, telephone, music, homework/academic achievement, interpersonal relations (including getting along with others), bedtime, and finances/spending. Although these topics are not unique to African American families, Smetana et al. did find differences between white and black Americans in how these conflicts unfold between parents and adolescents.

Conflict Processes and Outcomes

As with other parent–child groups, the more interesting questions to ask about cultural influences on parent–child conflict revolve around how these family members interact in conflict situations and what outcomes are associated with different processes. For example, Birditt et al. (2009) found that African American families were less likely to use avoidant strategies to resolve parent–adult child conflict than were European American families. They reasoned that this might reflect cultural differences between African Americans and European Americans in terms of emotional expressions and reliance on family ties. Other cultural differences in conflict processes have been found between American sub-groups as well. For example, Dixon et al. (2008) found that mother–daughter conflict was more intense in African American and Latino families when daughters' respect was low. However, the same intensity was not found when daughters in European American families had low levels of respect. Smetana et al. (2003) found that parent–adolescent conflict did not decrease in frequency or increase in intensity from early to middle adolescence, as has been found in studies of mostly European American families. Additionally, the longitudinal study by Smetana et al. indicated that African American P-C dyads tend to move from parent-unilateral modes of conflict resolution in early adolescence to more joint modes of conflict resolution in middle adolescence. However, the parent remains more authoritative in conflict situations in African American families than has been found in European American parent–adolescent dyads, perhaps indicating different cultural contexts for families.

Different ways of coping with cultural differences between parents and children are associated with different outcomes. For example, Ahn et al. (2009) examined cognitive flexibility and conflict outcomes when Korean American college students and their parents had differences in cultural values. They found that participants with high cognitive flexibility had more P-C conflict regarding dating and marriage when there were large values gaps compared to when there were small values gaps. However, this difference did not exist for participants with low cognitive flexibility. Ahn et al. (2009) reasoned that college students with high levels of cognitive flexibility might "unintentionally exacerbate" conflicts by the way they express their views to their parents, perhaps adopting Western notions of low power-distance and low context communication (that is, not seeing their parents as more powerful and not using indirect forms of expression that rely on context more for meaning).

Researchers also have studied how other aspects of parent–child relationships influence P-C conflict outcomes. For example, Choi et al. (2008) found that when clashes of cultural values occurred between Vietnamese and Cambodian immigrant parents and their adolescents, a high risk of problem behaviors for the adolescents emerged. However, parent–child bonding serves to buffer this outcome, consistent with other studies demonstrating the importance of considering relationship quality when drawing conclusions about conflict outcomes. Findings regarding supportive parent–child interactions were also found by Crean (2008), who studied associations between different parent–child dyads in Latino families, father and mother supportiveness, and child externalizing and internalizing behavior problems. For Latino adolescents in that study, boys' externalizing behaviors were altered by supportive parental relationships when they had high levels of conflict with the other parent. That is, mothers' supportiveness changed the link between father–son conflict and problem behavior just as fathers' supportiveness moderated the link between mother–son conflict. Unfortunately, only mother supportiveness moderated links between father–daughter conflict and behavior problems. Girls with high levels of conflict with their mothers displayed behavior problems but father supportiveness did not matter. As a whole, these studies indicate that we need to appreciate cultural elements, parent–child relationship qualities, conflict processes, and outcomes. In other words, parent–child relationships and how parents and children manage conflict vary in important ways across cultures.

Implications

First of all, family members, and professionals who work with them, can move toward positive conflict management by making the unexpected expected. By that we mean recognizing the "hot button" issues that arise with each developmental stage in the family life cycle and considering ways to manage those issues before they become points of contention. One critical notion is that the topic issues at each stage represent more than simply the content under current discussion. They also reflect the developmental processes that each person must go through. Understanding that fact will likely help the reader become more willing to engage in productive conflict communication with children. That awareness certainly will not eliminate parent–child conflict, but it will contribute to positive outcomes by allowing for planning to use constructive interactional tactics rather than knee-jerk reacting with negative tactics.

Some tactics identified in the literature as constructive include being willing to compromise, using reasoning, taking a problem-solving approach, and ensuring that nonverbal displays show positive emotions. Reviewing the tables in this chapter will remind readers that research is pretty clear that constructive strategies are linked to positive outcomes for children and families. On the flip side, these boxes remind us that negative conflict management strategies are linked to negative outcomes for children and families. Turning the unexpected into the expected can go a long way toward positive family outcomes.

Next, the findings about the prevalence of single-parent homes (about 40 percent) might come as a surprise. Women represent the vast majority of single parents, many of whom earn wages at or below the poverty level. The weight of working to support a child on one's own cannot be underestimated. That weight leads to both depression and stress in the parent which interferes with spending time doing routine activities. Conflict tends to be more negative and disruptive in single-parent families, despite the amount of love and energy that parents give to their children. Knowing the enormity of the challenges that single parents face should help frame an understanding of how they manage conflicts in the home.

Finally, parents and children increasingly occupy different cultural spaces as families develop over the lifespan. This occurs in immigrating as well as non-immigrating families. Constructive conflict processes in parent–child dyads take cultural values and orientations into account, understanding the increasingly complex cultural contexts of family systems. This is another unexpected aspect of family conflict that should be translated to the expected. Parents and children have the ability to construct positive relationship qualities that can buffer the stresses of cultural shifts within families. They would be wise to expect to do so.

5

Siblings in Conflict

She became furious and started yelling things like, "You love making people mad! You love causing arguments and conflicts! It makes you happy to do this, doesn't it?" I said that I didn't want to fight at all, but I wished she would have told me this before so we could have resolved it and clarified it earlier. Her words became more personal and hateful, so I interrupted, called her some names, and hung up the phone. She tried calling back but I knew it would get worse, so I didn't answer. Finally, I answered and asked what she wanted. She said I could never see her kids again and before I heard anything more, I hung up again.

Sibling relationships are a big part of family life. More importantly, sibling relationships are a big part of life in general, with approximately 80 percent of people having brothers and/or sisters (Dunn, 1983). Sibling relationships represent a unique type of peer relationship in that they are more obligatory than friends or romantic partners and they last longer than other relationships as well (Laursen et al., 2001; Mikkelson, 2006). As indicated by the opening account of one woman's conflict with her sister, siblings continue to engage in conflicts long after they stop living in the same home.

Because of the pervasive and unique nature of sibling relationships, family researchers have examined sibling conflicts and their consequences across the lifespan. This research has identified the important role that sibling conflict plays in children's social development. It also has examined associations between sibling conflict interactions and conflict with other family members (such as parent–child). Moreover, researchers have investigated specific topics, processes, and outcomes of sibling conflict in childhood and adolescence. We explore these issues in this chapter and summarize what we learn about managing the unexpected in sibling conflict across the lifespan. However, little empirical research has examined adult sibling conflict or differences in sibling conflict processes across cultures. We see these as areas ripe for future research and include brief discussions of these issues at the end of the chapter. First, we look at how unique characteristics of sibling relationships might influence ways brothers and sisters engage in conflicts.

What Makes Sibling Relationships Unique

Qualities of sibling relationships likely influence ways that siblings manage conflicts. Just as we discussed types of marriages, stepfamilies, and children of single parents (see chapters 2, 3, 4), different types of sibling relationships exist. Hetherington (1989) describes four types of sibling relationships: (1) *hostile and alienated relationships*, which are characterized by low warmth, low communication, high aggression, and high coercion; (2) *companiate-caring relationships*, which are characterized by high warmth, high communication, moderately low aggression, and moderately low rivalry; (3) *ambivalent relationships,* in which siblings are avoidant; and (4) *enmeshed relationships*, which exhibit the same patterns as companiate-caring relationships but in an unhealthy and restrictive way. These types reflect general relationship dimensions identified by other researchers, such as Stocker et al. (1997) who concluded that warmth, conflict, and rivalry likely characterize sibling relationships across the lifespan. In addition to these dimensions, siblings are different ages (except twins, of course), leading to inherent power differences not typically present in other peer relationships, such as friendships (Perlman & Ross, 2005). As we discuss later in the chapter, these age-based power differences influence sibling conflict interactions in interesting ways.

Siblings have a lot of conflict (Ram & Ross, 2008). However, conflict is different from siblings "fighting" and it is recognized as a separate issue from sibling rivalry (Stocker et al., 1997). Researchers often use the term *fighting* to depict when siblings are being aggressive or violent with each other. Shantz and Hartup (1992) noted that aggression is a sub-set of behaviors people might use to deal with conflict but should not be confused to be the same as conflict. *Rivalry* might not involve behavior at all, but rather includes thoughts and feelings of competition between siblings for attention, affection, and the like (Stocker et al., 1997). Sibling *conflict* includes *any incompatibility that can be expressed between siblings* (see chapter 1). As one can imagine, sisters and brothers have many opportunities to develop and express incompatibilities, from who gets the last popsicle in the box, to who gets to control the TV remote control, to whether their parent should move to an assisted living facility. Research indicates that many such conflicts recur and often do not get resolved (Ram & Ross, 2008). In fact, according to one study, four- and six-year-old siblings in their everyday household interactions have more than three disputes an hour; more than 80 percent of those conflicts end either without being resolved or with one of the siblings submitting to the other (Siddiqui & Ross, 1999, as cited in Recchia & Howe, 2009a).

One of the reasons siblings might be unmotivated to resolve conflicts is that a festering conflict is unlikely to end the relationship as it might with a friend (Laursen et al., 2001). For example, Laursen et al. reviewed 31 studies of peer conflict. They found that sibling conflict interactions were different from other peer conflict interactions in several ways. The most notable difference was that other peer relationships involve increases in constructive negotiation and decreases in coercion as people move from childhood into adolescence. The increase in constructive negotiation behaviors and decrease in destructive coercion behaviors did not emerge for sibling relationships. Furthermore, that review of studies revealed that adolescents more often resolve conflicts with their siblings by disengaging from the conflict than by negotiating a solution.

Although sibling conflicts, and sibling relationships in general, can be seen as training grounds for other peer relationships, competing theories explain associations between sibling and other peer relationships. Lockwood et al. (2001) point out that the *carryover model* predicts that sibling and peer relationship qualities are similar and children will interact in similar ways across these different relationships. In this case, a girl who has cold and contentious interactions with her sister will also have cold and contentious interactions with other peers. On the other hand, the *compensation model* predicts that these relationships will display different qualities as one relationship type compensates for a lack in the other type of relationship. In this case, a girl who has cold and contentious interactions with her sister will have warm and supportive interactions with other peers.

Unfortunately, research has not consistently shown support for one model over the other, and Lockwood et al. (2001) note that associations between sibling relationship qualities and other peer relationship qualities, including conflict, are more complex. For example, the Lockwood et al. study of links between sibling conflict and peer relationships at school found that children with low-conflict sibling relationships had lower social status in their classrooms, were more withdrawn, and were more likely to be victimized relative to children with high-conflict sibling relationships. However, children with high-conflict sibling relationships were more likely to be rejected by peers (2001, p. 63). These results indicate that either too much or too little sibling conflict could be detrimental to children's relationships outside the family. On the one hand, children who do not have enough sibling conflict do not have opportunities to develop social interaction skills. On the other hand, children who have too much conflict might develop defensive or aggressive interpersonal skills that lead to rejection by others. One way to unpack this complexity is to look at the role of conflict interactions in child development.

Sibling Conflict and Child Development

One of the reasons sibling conflict has gathered so much research attention, particularly in early childhood and adolescence, involves the potential implications these interactions have for other aspects of people's lives. Our earliest experiences with interpersonal conflict occur in the family, and particularly in sibling relationships, which we noted above provide a unique type of peer relationship not offered by parents or friends (Perlman et al., 2007). These peer relationships offer "opportunities to hone conflict resolution skills that are unavailable in other relationships" (Laursen et al., 2001, p. 424). Sibling conflict interactions have the potential to help children develop several important social functions, such as perspective-taking skills, consideration of others' feelings and beliefs, the ability to reflect about their internal states, negotiation, compromise, persuasion, and turn-taking (Brody, 1998; Foote & Holmes-Lonergan, 2003).

The difference between benefit and detriment seems to lie in the strategies and tactics used in managing conflicts over time. The level of emotional intensity involved also separates constructive from destructive conflicts, with constructive conflicts characterized by low emotional intensity and destructive conflicts characterized by high levels of emotional intensity (Howe et al., 2002). Beneficial sibling conflict interactions linked to warm and positive family relationships include negotiation or compromise, mutual self-assertion, and discussion (Brody, 1998; Howe et al., 2002; Ram & Ross, 2001). These types of interaction behaviors foster children's abilities to use these communication skills in other relationships as well. On the other hand, detrimental sibling conflict interactions linked to hostile and negative family relationships include prolonged conflicts that spread beyond the initial issue and are resolved either through sheer insistence or coercion (Howe et al., 2002; Ram & Ross, 2001). Such destructive sibling conflict connects to a host of undesirable child outcomes, including delinquent behaviors (such as property damage), internalizing problems (such as depression), and externalizing problems (such as aggressiveness) (Perlman et al., 2007). We discuss these processes and outcomes for particular age groups in the following sections.

Importantly as well, one must consider the entire family system when identifying links between sibling conflict and child development (Socha & Yingling, 2010). Garcia et al. (2000) pointed out that the *additive risk model* predicts that "children who experience conflictual relationships with both parents and siblings in the home are more likely to demonstrate aggressive behavior at home and in school" (p. 51). The reader will notice that this prediction is for "conflictual relationships" and not simply for the presence of conflict. That is, family relationships that often exhibit the destructive qualities discussed above would fall into the category of "conflictual relationships," but those relationships with constructive qualities discussed above would not. Brody (1998) noted that individual family member characteristics influence sibling conflict in addition to other subsystem relationship dynamics, such as interparental and parent–child relationships. Research has consistently shown that conflict management strategies across family relationships impact children's social development. For example, when parent–child relationships contain a high degree of positivity, such as constructive conflict interactions, sibling relationships also contain a high amount of positivity and prosocial behaviors, such as sharing, compromising, and the like (Brody, 1998). Likewise, parent–child relationships that include high levels of negativity and over-control coincide with sibling relationships that have a high level of aggressive, self-protective behaviors (Brody, 1998). Although these relationship qualities concern more than conflict interactions, conflict management strategies used throughout the family system influence sibling conflict management behaviors.

As we noted in chapters 3 and 4, strategies and tactics parents use to manage their own conflicts affect children in profound ways, often through the process of *spillover*. The reader will recall that this process involves the transfer of behaviors or emotions from one setting (or relationship) to another. So, for example, when a mother and father manage conflicts between themselves by shouting, the same tactic will likely be used when these parents have conflicts with their children. Research has found that interparental and parent–child conflict management processes also influence ways children manage conflicts with their siblings. For instance, children whose parents use other-oriented arguments and collaborative problem solving with their children tend to use more compromising and less verbal aggression in conflicts with their peers (Perlman et al., 2007). On the other hand, children whose parents use self-oriented arguments, power, or permissiveness in their parent–child conflicts tend to be less adaptive and more antagonistic in their peer conflict management (Perlman et al., 2007).

To understand further the associations between sibling conflict processes and outcomes, we devote the rest of the chapter to discussing specific age cohorts. As with parent–child conflict, most research on sibling conflict has focused either on early childhood or on adolescence. In keeping with a lifespan perspective, we first discuss what we know about sibling conflict interactions in early- to mid-childhood and then we discuss adolescent sibling conflict.

Sibling Conflict in Childhood

Children make dramatic advances in their social interaction skills in early childhood. One important, and pervasive, type of social interaction is conflict management. Several themes emerge in the research about childhood sibling conflict. First, researchers have identified common topics about which siblings have conflict. Research also provides valuable information about conflict management processes between young siblings. Related to processes, another theme concerns the role that development plays in conflict processes, including the role that birth order plays in sibling conflict. A final theme in childhood sibling conflict research is parental involvement. We discuss each of these themes below and then discuss connections between childhood sibling conflict processes and the next stage, adolescent sibling conflict.

Conflict Topics

Brothers and sisters argue over a variety of topics during childhood. As the reader can imagine, age plays a role in what conflict topics arise. For example, preschoolers tend to argue over toys

Table 5.1 Childhood Conflict Topic Categories

Conflict Topic	Example
Destructive behavior	Breaking a toy
Fairness/sharing	Dividing up a snack
Household chores	Cleaning up after playing
Independence	Building a Lego structure by oneself
Negotiating plans for play or pretense	Who will be the parent in a game of "house"
Personal space	Being allowed to play alone in room
Physical aggression	Hitting
Toys, possessions/ownership	Playing with a new toy
Taking turns	Taking turns on the swing
Teasing and joking	Using an undesired nickname

Adapted from Randell and Peterson (2009), p. 870

and other property (Randell & Peterson, 2009), which makes intuitive sense considering the daily life of a preschooler revolving around play. Interestingly, possessions continue to give rise to sibling conflict in elementary-aged children (Recchia & Howe, 2009a), although teasing and name-calling enter the scene as siblings get older. Sibling conflicts are not limited to arguments over toys, electronics, and other possessions. Some researchers have divided conflict topics into broad domains. Recchia and Howe list three main domains: (1) *moral conflicts*, which include physical harm (e.g., hitting), psychological harm (e.g., teasing), and fairness/rights violations (e.g., taking other's property); (2) *conventional conflicts*, which include rules/norms that may vary from one context to another (e.g., politeness); and (3) *personal conflicts*, which include preferences and privacy (e.g., personal space). Other researchers have identified more specific topics. For example, Randell and Peterson (2009) identified 10 sibling conflict topics. Table 5.1 lists these 10 topics, which represent conflicts identified by siblings, parents, and researchers. Recchia and Howe (2009a) noted that most sibling conflicts during childhood revolve around moral issues such as fairness (taking turns), welfare (physical or psychological harm), and rights (possessions or personal space). We find through these conflicts opportunities for moral development and lessons in morality within the family.

Conflict Management Processes

Research of sibling conflict during childhood typically includes observations of children's interactions (e.g., Howe et al., 2003; Perlman & Ross, 2005; Ram & Ross, 2001, 2008). These studies provide great benefit to understanding sibling conflict because they do not rely on recall by participants (which can be inaccurate) and they do not rely on a certain level of language skills by children. Observers can watch two-year-olds work through conflicts over possessions with siblings the same way they can watch six-year-olds work through those conflicts. Another benefit of these studies is they reflect a developmental approach to conflict, investigating associations of various conflict management tactics, strategies, and outcomes without biasing participants to view conflict as inherently bad or harmful. These studies typically watch and record how children of various ages work through conflict issues, such as dividing up toys or going through everyday household interactions.

For example, Ram and Ross (2001, 2008) conducted two studies that invited young children to come to an agreement about how to divide small toys between them that they could take home from the study. In the first study, six toys were to be divided among siblings who were either a four- and six-year-old dyad or a six- and eight-year-old dyad (Ram & Ross, 2001). In the second study, siblings (ages for younger siblings $M = 5.6$ years; ages for older siblings $M = 7.8$ years) were given only five toys, so there could not be an easy "3-3" solution (Ram & Ross, 2008). Both studies included instructions to come up with a solution that they could agree upon, which admittedly is not always the case in "real-life" sibling conflicts. Nevertheless, these laboratory interactions point to some interesting lessons in how young children manage conflict. First, *problem solving* emerged in both studies as the most frequently used conflict management strategy. This strategy represents "attempts to locate and adopt alternatives that satisfy both children's goals" (Ram & Ross, 2008, p. 518). Problem solving includes specific tactics such as giving information, asking questions, and guiding the division. Children also used *contention* to resolve the toy division conflict, but significantly less than problem solving. This strategy represents "attempts to persuade the other to concede, and refusals to concede to the other" (Ram & Ross, 2008, p. 518). Contentious tactics include messages such as stating positions and making persuasive arguments. The least-used strategy among these young siblings was *struggle*, which represents "attempts at withdrawing from the negotiation, or aggressive forms of contentious behavior including physical and verbal aggression" (Ram & Ross, 2008, p. 518). Struggle includes behaviors such as threats and negative evaluations.

Because these children were instructed to consider the other person in their solutions, and constructive problem solving emerged as the most common strategy, these studies point to a tip for fostering constructive sibling conflict: Tell siblings they need to find an agreeable decision and they likely will find one. Table 5.2 lists conflict management strategies and tactics observed by Ram and Ross in these studies of childhood sibling conflicts. As table 5.2 lists, the specific behaviors listed under problem solving include interaction skills identified earlier as benefits of sibling conflict. On the other hand, behaviors listed under contention and struggle include conflict tactics generally associated with a destructive strategy. Similarly, Ross et al. (2006) found that siblings who reached mutually beneficial resolutions in conflict interactions used constructive behaviors such as seeking agreement and having future-oriented discussions rather than getting stuck on accusations and past behavior.

Importantly, relationship qualities also influence conflict management processes between siblings. For instance, Ram and Ross (2001) found that when siblings had high conflicts of interest (i.e., they both strongly desired the same toy), they used fewer problem-solving tactics and more contentious tactics. Additionally, when siblings experienced these high conflicts of interest in negative relationships, they were not likely to reach a solution or resolve their differences. Siblings also tend to reciprocate behaviors during conflict (Perlman & Ross, 2005). For example, if one child is calm

Table 5.2   Childhood Sibling Strategies and Tactics

Strategy	Tactic	Example
Problem-	Informational Statements	"I want the ball."
solving	Guiding the Division	"And you take the frog pad."
	Propose Alternative Solutions	"Let's do rock paper scissors."
	Asking Questions	"Which one do you want?"
	Concession	"Okay."
	Other-oriented Arguments	"Cuz you like to do crafts."
Contention	Positional Statements	"I'm taking this one home!"
	Persuasive Arguments	"Cause I'm the oldest."
	Commands for Compliance	"You gotta yell."
	Refusal and Protesting	"No, you can't."
Struggle	Aggressive Verbal Moves	"You're going to cheat you cheater."
	Aggressive Physical Moves	Throws the objects on the floor.
	Inaction and Withdrawal	Walking away.
	Crying	

Adapted from Ram & Ross (2008), p. 518

and gives information about what she wants, her brother is more likely to also be calm and give information about what he wants. Unfortunately, the opposite case also occurs. If one child opens a conflict interaction with aggression, her sibling is likely to respond in like manner. Older siblings tend to carry more weight in this pattern than younger siblings, which we will discuss later, but the important lesson here is that siblings learn from each other and tend to keep behavior patterns going through reciprocation.

Developmental Influence on Sibling Conflict

Researchers have also focused on sibling interactions between toddlers, preschoolers, and elementary-aged children to identify developmental changes in conflict management processes. Earlier we pointed to the role that sibling conflicts play in children developing interaction skills they use in other relationships. As one can imagine, developmental levels of children also influence their sibling conflict interactions. When comparing toddlers, preschoolers, and elementary-aged children, interesting differences emerge that indicate the important role of child development in sibling conflict interactions.

Children demonstrate developmental maturity in their sibling conflicts through the use of other-oriented arguments and messages (see table 5.2). These include comments that consider the other child's position and interests, such as, "I know you want to watch that show," or "If I go first, then you will get to have the rest of the time." These types of messages appear more frequently in older sibling conflicts (e.g., 6–10-year-olds) than in younger sibling conflicts (e.g., 2–4-year-olds) (Recchia & Howe, 2009b; Ram & Ross, 2001). Just as sibling conflicts give children opportunities to "try out" interaction skills and refine those skills through practice, siblings increase their use of constructive strategies as they get older. This finding, that children use more constructive conflict strategies with age, can encourage parents who cringe at the frequency of sibling conflict. Related to this, Ram and Ross (2008) found that siblings who had opportunities to share information about what each child wanted before starting to negotiate a solution were able to negotiate more equitable solutions to their conflicts of interest. The lesson here is that before children can construct other-oriented messages to manage conflicts, they need to *know* what the other's position is. This is where we can see the value of discussion coming into sibling conflict management and the potential role for parental involvement.

A correlate to the developmental increase in other-oriented messages is an increase in the complexity of conflict interactions and a decrease in non-productive tactics such as crying, ignoring, and aggression (Perlman et al., 2007; Ram & Ross, 2001; see table 5.2). For example, Perlman et al. found that younger sibling dyads (2- and 4-year-olds) had more conflicts than they had two years later (as 4- and 6-year-olds). However, conflicts lasted longer than they did in the early years, pointing to more complex and sophisticated interaction skills. Although sibling conflicts persist throughout age cohorts, children mature from preschool into early elementary school so they learn how to "use their words" rather than their tears or their fists. That is, comparing older children (6- or 8-year-olds) to younger children (2- or 4-year-olds) reveals that older children rely less on crying and aggression and more on questioning and cooperation (Ram & Ross, 2001). These findings show a clear influence of child development on sibling conflict management, and provide encouragement for parents who find themselves constantly repeating, "Use your words" to their preschoolers!

A final theme in the research concerning developmental links to sibling conflict introduces the concept of *theory of mind*. Theory of mind refers to how people understand that "behavior is influenced by mental states" (Randell & Peterson, 2009, p. 857). This understanding is usually developed in early childhood, with research finding that children have greater theory of mind understanding when their families discuss thoughts and feelings (see Randell & Peterson for a review). Research indicates clear links between sibling conflict management and ways young children understand connections between thought and behavior (Foote & Holmes-Lonergan, 2003; Randell & Peterson, 2009; Selman, 1980). For example, Randell and Peterson (2009) found that children who had high theory of mind scores also engaged in amicable sibling conflicts that resulted in little or no distress. Similarly, Foote and Holmes-Lonergan (2003) found that preschoolers in their study who scored higher for theory of mind tended to use other-oriented arguments in their sibling conflicts and were more likely to understand the emotional perspectives of their siblings. These findings again point to the importance of discussion and child development in sibling conflict processes and outcomes. Children who can both separate thought from action and see how thought influences behavior demonstrate more constructive conflict management strategies and experience more productive outcomes.

Birth order effects

As the reader may have experienced when growing up, developmental influences also mean that older siblings tend to have the upper hand in sibling conflicts. With a developmental edge over their younger siblings, older siblings tend to take the behavioral lead when it comes to conflict management processes (Garcia et al., 2000; Howe et al., 2002; Perlman & Ross, 2005; Ram & Ross, 2001, 2008; Ross et al., 2006). As one might expect, younger siblings mimic older sibling behavior more than the reverse (Garcia et al., 2000). Importantly, this dominance in conflict processes can be either constructive or destructive. For example, when older siblings demonstrate problem-solving tactics such as other-oriented messages, asking questions, and suggesting alternatives, they take the lead in conflict management as well as modeling constructive conflict management tactics for their younger siblings. On the other hand, when older siblings use aggression or power moves, younger siblings tend to respond with opposition, crying, or appealing to a third party such as a parent (Perlman et al., 2007). Although younger siblings do not tend to reciprocate such aggression toward their older siblings, they can turn around and use such destructive tactics on another younger sibling!

As one would expect from this dominance, older siblings tend to benefit more from sibling conflicts, getting their way either by guiding the process, using more sophisticated tactics, or through aggression. For example, the dialogue below from Phinney (1986, p. 55) illustrates this power imbalance between the older sibling, David (6½ years old), and his younger sister, Judith (5 years old):

Speaker	Message
David:	Remember, this is my tent, isn't it?
Judith:	And mine.
David:	No, I just let you have it, don't I, to share.
Judith:	It's mine too.
David:	No, I just share it with you.
Judith:	Yes, and when you share it, it's mine with yours. Both together, it's ours.
David:	Yes, but I'm in charge here 'cause it was mine.
Judith:	I helped Mummy put it up. Does that matter to you?
David:	No.

Although David models reasoning as they negotiate ownership of the tent, it is clear that his position as the oldest and first owner of the tent will prevail regardless of Judith's arguments about shared ownership.

Sex differences

While examining birth order effects, several researchers also have investigated the role of gender in childhood sibling conflict, particularly as gender composition of sibling dyads might influence the process. Although many people assume that boys and girls interact differently, actual observations of sibling conflict interactions reveal very little difference. Overall, few sex differences emerge in these studies of actual behavior when examining differences between girls and boys (e.g., Ram & Ross, 2001, 2008; Randell & Peterson, 2009; Stocker et al., 2002). Two studies did find that younger brothers tended to be more aggressive and adversarial than younger sisters when having conflicts with older sisters (Howe et al., 2002; Recchia & Howe, 2009a), but such differences are not apparent when the older sibling is a boy. It seems that sisters and brothers are similarly capable and prone to engage in both constructive and destructive conflicts.

Parent Involvement

At several points in this chapter, we noted suggestions or benefits for parental involvement in childhood sibling conflict. Here we discuss parental involvement more, noting the complexities of such involvement. As one might expect, outcomes of parental involvement differ based on the type of involvement and ages of the siblings. Most research about parental involvement applies to mothers rather than fathers because mothers tend to participate in research more than fathers. When mothers intervene in their children's conflicts with punishments (e.g., "Stop right now or you will find yourselves in your rooms!") or self-oriented reasoning (e.g., "I can't take this anymore! Stop fighting!"), later sibling conflicts do not tend to be constructive (Recchia & Howe, 2009b). On the other hand, when mothers intervene using other-oriented reasoning and guide children to come to their own solutions (e.g., "I know you both want to work this out"), later sibling conflicts tend to be constructive (Recchia & Howe, 2009b). These con-clusions should not be surprising, given the spillover between parental conflict behavior and child conflict behavior discussed previously. However, maternal involvement can backfire, too. Some research indicates that when mothers get involved, their children will continue to seek their intervention through "third party" strategies in later conflicts (Howe et al., 2003). Ultimately, one would hope children could reap all the developmental ben-efits from sibling conflict experiences we discussed earlier in the chapter. Too much maternal involvement, or the wrong kind, could simply lead to kids who "go get Mom" whenever disputes arise. Kramer et al. (1999) concluded that parental involvement is probably more effective for younger children than for older chil-dren. Toddlers and preschoolers clearly need guidance in how to constructively manage the many sibling conflicts they experience in a given day. However, as children and their siblings develop social skills, parents should be less quick to jump in and help with sibling conflicts. Suggestions to siblings to find mutually agreeable solutions and encouragements to use problem-solving tactics are more beneficial in the long run than heavy-handed influence that demands a particular solution.

Outcomes of Childhood Sibling Conflict

Although there are many benefits children derive from managing their sibling conflicts in childhood, no simple relationship exists between the presence of sibling conflict and behaviors later in life. As we have noted throughout this discussion, outcomes relate much more to *how* sibling conflict is managed, because it is inevitable that sibling conflict *will* occur. For example, Garcia et al. (2000) exam-ined sibling conflict processes when boys were 2 years old and then followed up with those boys when they were 5- and 6-year olds. They wanted to see if links occur between ways siblings interact during conflicts and behavior problems later. They found that boys who had aversive and aggressive conflict interactions with their sib-lings at an early age more likely displayed behavior problems, such as fighting, acting out, and breaking rules, when they were 5 and

6 years old. This study also looked at the additive effect of rejecting parenting practices by mothers (such as criticizing or having hostile mannerisms). They found that problem behaviors increased when boys had destructive conflict interactions with their siblings and also experienced rejection from their mothers. Here again we see the importance of modeling constructive conflict management behaviors by both older siblings and parents.

Childhood sibling conflict continues to influence children as they move into adolescence. Stocker et al. (2002) found that the more conflict 10-year-olds had with their brothers or sisters, the more anxiety, depression, and delinquent behavior they had two years later. Furthermore, the more conflict siblings had when children were 10 years old, the more conflict they had two years later as well. Bullock et al. (2002) also followed families from when children were 10 years old into early adolescence and then into young adulthood. Results from their study showed that children who had highly critical siblings and who experienced high destructive sibling conflict (such as aggressiveness) had a higher likelihood of having later problems with delinquency, substance use, and criminal arrest. Although these longitudinal studies did not observe actual everyday conflict interactions or examine conflict management strategies, children nevertheless take their sibling conflict interactions with them as they move out of childhood and into adolescence, a phase of family life that is full of contention in its own right. The following section discusses adolescent sibling conflict in more detail.

Adolescent Sibling Conflict

As the reader can attest, adolescence is a time when the hormones rage and relationships come along for the ride. As mentioned in chapter 4, adolescence constitutes a critically important time for one to seek one's personal identity and expansion outside the family. As Feinberg et al. (2003) noted, "Adolescence is typically a period in which children explore the roles and identities beyond those ascribed to them by their families" (p. 1262).

Adolescent sibling conflicts of a negative nature can adversely affect a person's adjustment. Bank et al. (2004) found that conflict in early adolescence predicted activity in deviant behavior (e.g., stealing at school, vandalism) when the child was in mid-adolescence. Consistent with the additive risk model discussed above, Bank et al. concluded that P-C conflict and sibling conflicts constitute two separate subsystems that combine to "amplify the risk for antisocial behavior . . . at the transition to adolescence" (p. 117). Likewise, Sherman et al. (2006) found that adolescent well-being connected to whether their sibling relationships were harmonious (low conflict, high warmth) or affect-intense (high conflict, high warmth). Siblings in the harmonious group were better off than those in the affect-intense group. Feeling warmth toward someone who continually opposes you can result in depression and a negative sense of well-being.

Moreover, negative conflict behaviors lead to negative family relationships. Using negative conflict tactics decreases other family members' confidence in their knowledge of the person using the negative tactics (Avtgis, 2003). Negative conflicts adversely affect family cohesion and other positive family characteristics up to a year later (Brody et al., 1992). Not surprisingly, ongoing and negative sibling conflicts tempt parents to intervene, at times showing favoritism to one of the siblings (Brody et al., 1992).

As mentioned earlier, "siblings usually differ in age, are bound by involuntary ties, and may or may not like each other as individuals" (Raffaelli, 1997, p. 540). Accordingly, adolescents may want to differentiate themselves from their siblings. Interestingly, the closer in age two siblings are, the greater the desire for differentiation (Feinberg et al., 2003). Given that many siblings are often only between 2 and 3 years apart in age, a need for differentiation by the older sibling can represent a hidden reason for sibling conflicts. This need for differentiation helps explain why children in early adolescence report more sibling conflicts than do their younger siblings (e.g., Campione-Barr & Smetana, 2010) and engage in fewer activities with their younger brothers and sisters (Cole & Kerns, 2001).

As we discussed with childhood siblings, adolescent siblings tend to mirror each other's good or bad interaction behaviors (Rinaldi & Howe, 1998). In terms of modeling one's sibling, Gamble et al. (2011) found that modeling can increase one's internalization and externalization problems, most critically when the siblings rely on negative conflict behaviors. Even older siblings who model their younger siblings can have adjustment problems to the extent negative conflict tactics are used with that sibling (Gamble et al., 2011).

Frequencies and Topics of Conflict

How frequent is adolescent sibling conflict? Estimates of adolescent sibling conflict vary according to the adolescent's age. Some studies show that the frequency of sibling conflict increases from childhood to early adolescence; then it tapers off (Burmester & Furman, 1990; Kim et al., 2006; see also Collins & Laursen, 1992). Kim et al. (2006) found that sibling conflict peaks at approximately 13 years of age (for the older sibling) and then declines over the years. The reliance on negative conflict tactics also appears to peak at middle adolescence and to taper during late adolescence (Reese-Weber, 2000).

In addition, many adolescent sibling conflicts can become habitual – that is, they continue without resolution. In one study, girls reported that one-third of their sibling conflicts are habitual (Raffaelli, 1997). Moreover, a positive association exists between the continuation of conflicts and use of destructive (but not constructive) conflict messages (Rinaldi & Howe, 1998). The reason for the positive link between ongoing conflicts and use of destructive tactics is straightforward – negative conflict tactics simply work against the mutual resolution of conflict.

One intriguing aspect of the occurrence of conflict involves the sex composition of the sibling dyad. Kim et al. (2006), for example, reported that sister–sister dyads tend to be the most harmonious and least conflictual compared to brother–brother dyads and mixed-sex dyads. Other research suggests that although boy–boy dyads are more aggressive than girl–girl dyads, more conflicts tend to occur in mixed-sex dyads (e.g., Vandell & Bailey, 1992). However, another study involving young adults found that mixed-sex siblings were less contentious than either boy–boy or girl–girl siblings (Stocker et al., 1997). In brief, the issue of conflict frequency remains tied to the age and sex composition of the siblings.

What do adolescent siblings argue about? The answer depends on how one slices the pie – into halves, quarters, or even smaller pieces. Campione-Barr and Smetana (2010) divided the pie into two large issues, which contained other topics of conflict. The first is the *personal domain*, and this concerns going into the other person's room, borrowing items without getting permission, hanging around the other sibling's friends, and so forth. The second set of conflict issues concerns matters of *equality*, such as who gets control over the TV remote, who gets to use the computer, taking turns riding in the front of the car, etc. These researchers found that conflicts about personal domain issues, but not equality, negatively associated with both older and younger sibling relational satisfaction with the sibling. These authors concluded that "it is likely that [conflicts about personal domain issues] reflect adolescents' basic needs to claim some issues as outside of legitimate control by others" (p. 469).

Dividing the topic pie into quarters, Raffaelli (1992, 1997) reported four major conflict issues. The first is about *power*, including such topics as controlling the other person's behavior and turn taking. *Personal property disputes* concern using items without permission and so forth. *Abusive* conflicts involve either psychological abuse (e.g., teasing) or physical abuse (e.g., hitting). Finally, *relational betrayal* refers to acting in a way that reduces trust or is neglectful. Consider the following example, which portrays one kind of power conflict:

> Yesterday, I had a few friends over and he wouldn't leave me alone. He kept coming in my room, picking on me, saying I was going to get in trouble for having people in the house, and he turned off my radio once or twice." (Raffaelli, 1992, p. 656)

Finally, McGuire et al. (2000) divided the conflict topic pie into 12 pieces. They relied on previous research and interviews

Table 5.3   Adolescent Conflict Topic Categories

Conflict Topic	Example
Aggression	
Physical	Hitting, throwing things
Verbal	Yelling, threatening
Teasing	Teasing comments, insults
Tattling	Telling on sibling to parent
Control	Controlling other sibling's behavior
Appropriate Behavior	Talking back to parents, lying
Sharing	
Common Objects	Sharing TV remote, taking turns
Personal Objects	Sharing one's own bike, computer
Friends	Sharing friends, teasing in front of friends
Rejection	Not wanting to play, walking away
Privacy	Needing personal space or time
Competition	Competing in games, sports, etc.
Rivalry	Seeking differential treatment by parents
Personality	Being immature, other negative attributes
General	Being in bad mood, being irritated

Adapted from McGuire et al. (2000), p. 17

with adolescents to derive their categories. Table 5.3 reports these behaviors. McGuire et al. (2000) found that older siblings mentioned lack of privacy, other child's irritability, and verbal aggression more as conflict topics. Younger siblings mentioned physical aggression more than did older siblings.

Overall, the most frequent topics for adolescent sibling conflict involve power and personal possessions (Collins & Laursen, 1992; McGuire et al., 2000; Raffaelli, 1997). However, by adolescence, conflicts about sibling rivalry largely disappear (McGuire et al., 2000). One might ask why personal property issues remain salient for adolescents. McGuire et al. (2000) speculated that personal possession conflicts are tied to "children's developing sense of self, social comparison, and positive justice as they deal with ownership and fairness" (p. 186). In other words, a valued possession represents a symbol of the adolescent's individuation and the right to their own possessions.

Conflict Management Processes

The lion's share of the literature on adolescent sibling conflict emphasizes two broad dimensions of behavior: positivity and negativity (Gamble et al., 2011). For example, Sherman et al. (2006) found that conflict is more powerful than warmth when predicting adolescents' well-being. Likewise, Updegraff et al. (2005) reported that siblings felt greater warmth and less negativity toward each other to the extent that aggression was not used (where aggression was found in direct and indirect tactics). As these terms imply, positivity includes such factors as warmth and affection; negativity contains aggression and conflict. These dual concerns are often examined in the same study, though the operationalizations for conflict tend to include only negative interaction behavior. As such, the information one might obtain from conflict between adolescent siblings does not take advantage of the full scope of conflict tactics that adolescents use that can affect outcomes, such as relational quality or adjustment (Collins & Laursen, 1992).

One reason conflict is treated as inherently negative could stem from the fact that adolescent sibling conflicts can be ruthless. Montemayor and Hanson (1985) document how over 60 percent of high-school seniors had hit a sibling the previous year. These authors observed that "the escalation of an aggressive attack reaches its highest intensity when the victim is a sibling, especially a younger one" (p. 24). Similarly, Raffaelli (1997) reported that adolescent sibling conflict "is the most frequent source of physical harm for youngsters" (p. 555). Consider the following interview excerpts, wherein two siblings tell their side of the story to the researcher:

Brother (13 years old): She [sister] yells at them [twin little brothers], tries to fight them or be mean to them, only like I said, she calls them names, bad names. She keeps hitting me and I don't want to hit her back. But, I need to so I could defend myself. She bugs me all the time when my cousins and my parents come, she bugs me and tries to like play with us. But because it's boys and a girl, so I tell her she should go with the parents. My parents will say that uh, not to hit your brothers, or be mean because . . . My parents say if [sister] hits me, I might have to hit her back and she's gonna cry. And she um, she's too stubborn. Then [the twin little brothers], they're little kids. They're not like big, like us.

Sister (11 years old): Like my big, like my little brothers, always yell or tell my dad and I get in trouble because I hit them or do something back to them and he hits me back. I mean he always tells – my big brother – he always hits me and then I hit him and then I tell my dad that he's hitting me and stuff. And they say, like, "Don't fight with your brothers."

We know that alternative conflict strategies exist; destructive aggression offers only one (and a poor one at that) strategic option for adolescent siblings.

One study examined four different conflict strategies that early adolescents employ. Rinaldi and Howe (1998) interviewed 11-year-olds and observed their interactions with siblings. They coded the frequencies of four conflict strategies, approximately 60 percent of which were direct and negative. The most common strategy used was *destructive* (used 40 percent of the time). This strategy contained such behaviors as direct and negative verbal and nonverbal statements, and withdrawal. Twenty-three percent of the time, adolescents relied on *prosocial tactics*. These included disclosure, admiration, and signs of warmth. Next, *equity* was used 19 percent of the time. Using equity tactics, one would attempt to dominate the other, compete with the other, and so forth. Finally, siblings used *constructive tactics* only 17 percent of the time. These tactics included compromise, reconciliation, collaboration/problem solving, and the like (similar to *negotiation* tactics presented earlier).

In a similar manner, Montemayor and Hanson (1985) found that siblings relied most on withdrawal (e.g., leave the scene), followed by an authoritarian strategy (e.g., commands the person to do something), followed by negotiation tactics (e.g., offer a compromise). Likewise, Raffaelli (1992) found that approximately 37 percent of conflicts were marked by withdrawal; capitulation occurred 28 percent of the time; parents intervened 27 percent of the time, and compromise was used only 8 percent of the time. In short, the use of direct and positive constructive tactics appears to be rare.

Regardless, the least used conflict management strategy (the constructive strategy) is the most effective on a variety of fronts. For example, Rinaldi and Howe (1998) found that constructive tactics were positively associated with perceived warmth, and they correlated negatively with frequency of conflict. Destructive tactics correlated negatively with warmth and were positively associated with frequency of conflict. Equity tactics correlated positively with conflict frequency. Finally, prosocial tactics positively associated with perceived warmth, and they negatively associated with frequency of conflict. The authors interpreted their findings to mean that children who rely on constructive tactics in particular during "conflicts with their siblings are able to work through their disagreements without hindering the positive feelings that exist between them" (p. 417).

In a similar vein, Pawlowski et al. (2000) examined how different conflict strategies connect to larger relational dimensions. More precisely, they examined how *integrative tactics* (compromise, collaborate, problem solve, etc.), *distributive tactics* (intimidate, use sarcasm, etc.), and *avoidance tactics* (e.g., change topic, avoid topic) associated with perceptions of desired relational dimensions such as relational immediacy, similarity, receptivity, task-involvement, and so forth. They found that the use of integrative conflict tactics connected to the positive dimensions of immediacy, similarity, and receptivity. However, use of distributive tactics negatively correlated with perceptions of the positive relational dimensions. Avoidance was negatively associated with being immediate and with task-orientation. These findings indicate the importance of conflict management tactics to adolescent sibling relationships across a broad span of desired relational dimensions.

Finally, third-party involvement, usually by parents, represents one common way that adolescent sibling conflicts end (McGuire et al., 2000). Raffaelli (1997) reported that siblings more likely than friends experience third-party involvement. Apparently, siblings often pursue conflicts until a third-party somehow becomes involved (Raffaelli, 1997). As conflicts increase in negativity, the more likely parents are to get involved (Brody et al., 1992).

As discussed above concerning parent involvement in childhood conflicts, different styles of third-party involvement exist. Milevsky et al. (2011) reported on three parental involvement styles. *Non-involvement* includes ignoring the problem, telling the siblings to work it out themselves, etc. *Coaching* concerns giving advice, indicating what the sibling was thinking, and so forth. Finally, *intervention* concerns stepping in and stopping the conflict. Milevsky et al. (2011) found that coaching tends to work best, especially with a same-sexed child (i.e., father–son, mother–daughter). And coaching, in contrast to intervention, connects to higher perceptions of warmth. Moreover, Updegraff et al. (2005) found that maternal intervention actually increased daughters' (but not sons') use of aggression, but that paternal intervention can reduce aggression. Updegraff et al. argued that fathers relate to children in terms of leisure activities and are thus more relevant to the kinds of activities that might lead to conflict (e.g., playing games or competitive sports).

As the opening vignette indicates, adolescents typically continue relationships with their siblings into adulthood and therefore continue to have opportunities for conflict. Unfortunately, research does not reflect this relational continuation. There is a noticeable lack of research about sibling conflict communication in adult life (Mikkelson, 2006). Although a few researchers have studied college students as "young adults," the average ages of study participants tend to fall in the late-adolescent range, so we have included lessons learned from that research in this section (e.g., Pawlowski et al., 2000; Sherman et al., 2006; Stocker et al., 1997). Another issue of sibling conflict that has not garnered much research attention is cultural influences and differences. This is consistent with a dearth of culturally inquisitive research across family communication domains (Diggs & Socha, 2004). One study provides interesting information about cultural influences on sibling conflict processes, so we highlight those findings in the following section.

Cultural Influences on Sibling Conflict

Killoren et al. (2008) studied Mexican American adolescent siblings to understand how cultural orientations influence family communication processes. Rather than taking a "national culture" approach that might not identify important cultural dimensions of family life (Oetzel et al., 2003), Killoren et al. (2008) asked Mexican American teens about their orientations toward Anglo and Mexican cultures. They also asked about the importance of familism when they asked them to report on strategies used in conflicts experienced with their siblings. Familism constitutes a strong value in Mexican culture, relating to feelings of obligation to one's family, the view that one's behavior reflects on the family as a whole, among other things (Killoren et al., 2008). As one might predict from individualistic and competitive orientations of the Anglo-American culture, adolescents with Anglo orientations used more controlling strategies. However, participants who rated familism values highly used more solution-oriented and non-confrontation strategies. The researchers also found an unexpected result: Adolescents who reported bicultural orientations, meaning they identified with *both* Anglo and Mexican cultural dimensions, tended to use more solution orientation in their sibling conflicts than did adolescents who only identified with one culture. Bicultural orientation refers to a constructive cultural adaptation strategy and these results indicate that it also links to sibling constructive conflict. This study provides insights into the role of culture in family conflict processes, and specifically sibling conflict processes. It also indicates that much remains to be known about the relationship between broad cultural factors and ways siblings manage their conflicts.

Implications

Opportunities for sibling conflict emerge shortly after a second child becomes part of a family system. Just as toddlers have conflicts with their parents, toddlers also have conflicts with their siblings. One of the unexpected findings from research, however, concerns how sibling conflict can be highly beneficial to children's overall social development. Although parents might be tempted to eliminate, or at least reduce, conflicts that arise between brothers and sisters, the brutal reality of family life concerns how sibling conflict is inevitable. A more realistic approach focuses on the developmental benefits of conflict and encourages children to use sibling interactions as "practice sessions" for honing skills of negotiation, perspective taking, information giving, and asking questions (also see Socha & Yingling, 2010).

In spite of the many potential benefits of sibling conflict, high levels of mismanaged sibling conflict can be detrimental to children's relationships with friends. Mismanaged sibling conflict can also lead to sibling relationships that have less warmth, intimacy, and support later in life. In other words, sibling conflict matters to relationships inside and outside the family as well as to well-being. Importantly, family members have much control over the outcomes of sibling conflict through ways they get involved in sibling conflicts. Older brothers and sisters greatly influence how conflicts play out with their younger brothers and sisters. When older siblings model constructive conflict behaviors, younger siblings tend to reciprocate those constructive behaviors. Such interactions, over time, lead to positive relationships. Parents also can both model constructive communication behaviors and encourage positive outcomes by the ways they handle their own conflicts and by the ways they intercede in their children's disputes.

Adolescent conflict reaches its zenith during early adolescence and depends on the sex composition of the siblings. Male siblings and cross-sex siblings tend to experience the most conflict, though cross-sex siblings can have the least amount of conflict once they reach adulthood. Maturity no doubt eases the animosity that might have been present years earlier, probably through more thoughtful ways of managing conflict.

Adolescent siblings tend to have conflicts about a variety of issues, though the most salient concern personal power and property. Having a sibling barge into one's room or take a possession without permission represents severe violations of one's identity and rights. The importance of such issues can easily be unanticipated, especially by the younger sibling who might not understand the developmental task that his or her adolescent sibling is undertaking. Also, the family as a whole might wonder why the older sibling suddenly tries hard to differentiate him- or herself from the family, neglecting the younger sibling in the process.

Adolescents tend to rely on destructive methods to manage conflict approximately 60 percent of the time, and their use of aggression is unnerving. The tendency for adolescent sibling conflict to be destructive might be unexpected. Moreover, adolescents tend not to rely on the most effective conflict management strategy: constructive tactics. The use of constructive and prosocial strategies appears much more productive (in terms of resolving the conflicts) and effective (in terms of relational quality and individual adjustment) when compared to the destructive tactics that appear too common.

Finally third-party involvement can help resolve conflict, escalate aggression, or inhibit future resolution efforts. The manner in which parents intercede can make all the difference. Simply intervening can be hazardous, probably because it does nothing to resolve the conflict. However, coaching appears to work better, by having an authority figure explain the whys and wherefores of each person's side, suggesting a course of mutual problem description and integration. Of course, parents do not often think of the form of involvement that might work best to resolve sibling conflict. Probably, parents mostly want the conflict between their children to stop. When asked to get involved, parents can provide an unexpected opportunity to their children of any age to forge mutually beneficial solutions themselves.

Now that we have discussed conflict in different family subsystems, we turn our attention in the next chapter to challenges that arise in family life. These challenges are often unexpected but more commonly experienced than one might think. We encourage the reader to consider what we have discussed concerning marital conflict (chapter 2), interparental, post-divorce, and stepfamily conflict (chapter 3), parent–child conflict (chapter 4), and sibling conflict (this chapter) as we explore the work–family interface and issues of health and disability in chapter 6.

6

Conflict in the Face of Family Challenges: Work–Family Interface, Health & Disability, and Family Resilience

Wife: Fairly soon after our children were diagnosed [with autism] I was doing some research and realized that my husband fit all the criteria for ADD and I was kind of like, "Oh, maybe that kind of explains something."

Husband: I had not been diagnosed.

Wife: He had not been diagnosed, had no idea what it was, and when I brought it to him he was just immensely offended 'cause it was like, "You have a problem and you're broken," and it was kind of like receiving a diagnosis for the kids, "You're disabled." And so it didn't go over very well. I was not popular.

Husband: I don't get upset very easily.

Wife: No he doesn't, he's very humble towards people who criticize him or anything like that and I wasn't bringing it as a, "You're broken" type of thing. But it was like, "Oh! Well that makes sense, you know, why some of these things are happening and why you do certain things the way you do." And my husband took it very personally.

Husband: My wife never does anything malicious. It wasn't meant maliciously. It wasn't meant as an attack.

Wife: It wasn't an attack.

Husband: And I had a history of learning from my mistakes. I don't make the same mistake twice. I don't think it was very long after, it didn't take –

Wife: About a month, I think, at least, maybe a month and a half, before you stopped being really grumpy with me about that.

Husband: Yeah. I just came to the realization that if this is something that I have then I better find out about it and take care of it. 'Cause I prefer to go forward.

Over the lifespan, family members deal with numerous challenges that affect their family interactions (Maguire, 2012). We cannot catalogue all such challenges here; rather, we discuss three aspects of family challenges that have garnered significant empirical attention as they relate to family conflict processes: The interface of work and family, chronic illnesses and disabilities, and family resilience. The first two issues represent unexpected, and ongoing, challenges families face. The third issue represents a positive approach to conflict processes in the face of unexpected family challenges.

Many of the concepts from earlier chapters are revisited in this chapter. Indeed, the previous chapters provide a good foundation for discussing the interplay of family conflict processes and challenges families face over the lifespan. This chapter provides examples of how scholars and practitioners apply family conflict theory and research to address important issues in family members' lives. Our hope is that these example issues will spark interest for innovative applications of family conflict concepts to other issues families face. We hope that by ending this book with a discussion of family resilience, readers are encouraged by the promise of positive approaches to family conflict studies.

Work–Family Interface

It has been quite interesting to observe the increased research attention paid to the interplay of work and family domains over the past couple of decades. Late in the twentieth century, family researchers began offering perspectives on connections between work life and family life. This research has moved beyond the myth of "balance" to reflect a more nuanced approach to the work–family interface (Kirby et al., 2006). Indeed, recent research focuses on the work–life interface in recognition that families are differentially central in workers' lives (Kirby et al., 2006). However, we use the term *work–family* because our purpose is to highlight ways this interface impacts (and is impacted by) family communication. For instance, some research differentiates between work→family conflict, which occurs when work roles/obligations conflict with fulfilling family roles/obligations, and family→work conflict, which occurs when family roles or obligations conflict with fulfilling work roles or obligations (e.g., Cinamon et al., 2007; Huang et al., 2004). Others have explored differences in how family members experience work–family conflict (e.g., Crouter et al., 1999; Kinnunen et al., 2010). A more recent approach, which we will discuss further at the end of the chapter, explores ways each domain might facilitate functioning in the other domain (e.g., Grzywacz & Bass, 2003).

Each of us has experienced work–family conflict to some extent. Many researchers adopt the definition offered by Greenhaus and Beutell (1985), which states work–family conflict (WFC) represents "a form of inter-role conflict in which the role pressures from the work and family domains are mutually incompatible to some respect" (p. 77). This definition is broad enough to allow people to explore various aspects of role pressures as well as factors of incompatibility. For example, Crouter et al. (1999) measured *role overload*, "the overwhelming feeling that it is difficult to accomplish everything that one needs to accomplish" (p. 1454), and *work pressure*, which included deadlines and a fast-paced work environment, as separate dimensions of WFC. Adopting a broad role-based definition of WFC also frees those who experience this conflict to understand it as perhaps a more normal, and to-be-expected (rather than unexpected), part of being members of both family and work systems. In this way we can begin to address ways in which WFC emerges, is experienced, and might be minimized for different family members.

Clearly, WFC is not an individual experience. Rather, the work–family interface can affect all family members, both individually and collectively (e.g., Crouter et al., 1999; Matthews et al., 2006). We see this impact in everyday family interactions including conflict interactions. For instance, Repetti (1994) examined how work affected the family life of male air traffic controllers. She found that pressures of work and poor relations at work led to more anger, less involvement, and more withdrawal from their children. Repetti concluded that "negative mood spillover may sometimes be both a short-term and long-term consequence of poor social relations at work" (p. 12). Likewise, Repetti and Wood (1997) observed mother–child interactions and assessed how the amount of stress affected mothers' levels of emotional involvement with their children after a day at work. They found that mothers with continually high levels of stress had more conflicts with their preschool children, were less involved emotionally, and were more controlling. However, Repetti and Wood also found that one group of mothers (who were not depressed or exhibit Type A behaviors of time urgency, competitiveness, and being easily upset) did not engage in negative or withdrawing behaviors with their children.

In one study of romantic partners, Green et al. (2011) examined associations between "work-interfering-with-family behaviors" (WIF) (p. 753), work–family conflict (WFC), and negative emotional displays in couples' interactions. They found that when the focal workers reported WIF behaviors, such as worrying about work, discussing work, and spending extra time doing work, their partners observed more WFC and also tended to engage in negative emotional displays (depression, unhappiness, fear, anxiety, worry, anger, and irritation) when the focal workers talked about work. Furthermore, the researchers assessed associations between WIF, WFC, and blame attributions. To assess blame attributions, the authors provided three scenarios about work keeping workers from fully participating in family functions or interactions. Partners assessed how much the worker was to blame. Results revealed that the more a partner saw WIF behaviors and WFC, the more likely she/he was to blame the worker for the scenario. Although this study did not specifically examine conflict interactions, this study helps us see the ripple effect of WFC on dyadic interactions in families. Over time, negative emotional displays and blame erode relationship quality and are bound to increase destructive conflict management strategies such as antagonism and fighting (see chapter 2).

Other research has found both work→family and family→work conflict affect other family relationships as well. Cinamon et al. (2007) found that both greater work→family conflict and greater family→work conflict associated with perceptions of lower quality parent–child interactions and a lower sense of parental effectiveness. Similarly, Crouter et al. (1999) found that mothers' and fathers' work pressures directly related to parents' reports of role overload. Parents' greater role overload was associated with higher levels of parent–adolescent conflict, and this conflict was directly related to adolescents' well-being. Clearly, the work–family interface is consequential for family conflict processes.

Several studies have investigated *crossover effects* of WFC, which "occur when an individual's personal experiences of stress, strain, and depression influence the other member of the relationship dyad" (Matthews et al., 2006, p. 229). Crossover effects are different than associations of WFC with family interaction dynamics or other outcomes, as in the studies discussed above. Rather, crossover effects refer to how effects in one person coincide with similar effects in another person. For instance, Cinamon et al. (2007) found crossover effects in that a higher rate of family→work conflict in one spouse was associated with a higher rate of work→family conflict in the other spouse and *vice versa*. Let's look at how this finding might translate to a real-life situation.

As the reader is well aware by now, we (the authors) are a dual-earner married couple. If the Cinamon et al. findings hold true in our family, the more Dan feels that family obligations (such as cooking dinner) get in the way of meeting his work obligations (such as writing this book), the more Heather is likely to feel that work obligations (such as writing this book) get in the way of meeting family obligations (such as gardening). Crouter et al. (1999) also found crossover effects in that fathers' work pressure was directly related to their own role overload *and* to mothers' role overload. That study found two ways for mothers to experience role overload, both through their own work pressures and from their husbands' work pressures. Recall from above that role overload was directly related to parent–child conflict, indicating that mothers had more factors contributing to conflict with their adolescent children than did fathers due to crossover effects. Other research has found similar sex differences in WFC experiences, which we discuss next.

Sex Differences in Work–Family Conflict

Although families increasingly include dual-earner couples, differences persist in how men and women in heterosexual couples experience work–family conflict. These differences have been found across countries and cultures, including but not limited to the United States (e.g., Crouter et al., 1999), the Middle East (e.g., Cinamon et al., 2007), East Asia (e.g., Lau, 2010), and Scandinavia (e.g., Kinnunen et al., 2010). For the most part, researchers explain these differences by asserting that traditional sex roles continue to function in families, leading women to experience more deleterious effects of WFC than men, even when objective measures of work and family demands are similar for partners. For example, Huang et al. (2004) found reciprocal relationships between work→family and family→work conflict for husbands and wives over time. However, associations between the two types of WFC from Time 1 to Time 2 were much stronger for wives than for husbands. For instance, the association between Time 1 family→work conflict accounted for a whopping 25 percent of the variation in Time 2 work→family conflict for wives. Referring to ourselves again, this type of association might play out in our family by both Dan and Heather feeling conflicts between meeting work and family obligations and over time we might see both domains getting in the way of each other. However, over time, Heather's feelings of family getting in the way of meeting work obligations will lead to *more* feelings of work getting in the way of family than would Dan's. Huang et al. (2004) note that we need to keep in mind that both types of WFC influence each other, but that these effects likely are different for men than for women. Findings from Kinnunen et al. (2010) support this assertion. Their study of working couples in Finland found that husbands reported higher levels of both types of WFC (work→family and family→work) at Time 1 and Time 2 but that wives were more likely than husbands to report parental distress at both times.

Traditional sex role expectations seem to explain associations between WFC and other relationship dynamics as well. Hill's (2005) study of working couples in the United States found that

fathers worked more hours and had work cultures less supportive of family life than did mothers; yet working fathers reported
less work–family conflict, less stress, and more satisfaction with
their families and marriages than did working mothers. Similarly,
Matthews et al. (2006) studied how men and women perceived
interferences between work and their relationships, what they
labeled "work-to-relationship conflict." In that study, they found
a direct crossover effect between work-to-relationship conflict
reported by women and relationship tension reported by men.
The more women reported that their work interfered with their
romantic relationships, the more their male partners reported
tension in those relationships. However, the *opposite* association
emerged with men's work-to-relationship conflict. That is, the
more men reported that their work interfered with their relationships, the *less* their female partners reported relationship tension.
These researchers reasoned that men and women in their study
likely had different expectations of what partners should bring to
relationships, with men expecting more attention to the relationship by women and women expecting less from men. Although
these traditional sex role expectations have been found in work–
family research across the globe, some cultural differences exist in
how families experience the interface between work and family
domains.

Culture and Work–Family Conflict

As with other aspects of family, expectations and values of
work, family, and the interface of the two domains are developed over time within particular sociocultural systems (Galovan
et al., 2010). Because the rise of dual-earner couples is a global
phenomenon, a few researchers have compared how people in
different cultures experience work–family conflict. For example,
Galovan et al. (2010) compared the association of WFC and
depression experienced by participants in the United States and
Singapore. Although they found a positive association between
WFC and depression in both countries, the results differed some-
what. Participants in the United States reported more depression

with work→family conflict than with family→work conflict, whereas participants in Singapore reported more depression with family→work conflict than with work→family conflict. The researchers proposed that this difference is based on the cultural differences between the two countries. That is, Singapore is a more collectivistic culture that values personal sacrifice (such as long work hours) for the benefit of the family, and the United States is a more individualistic culture that values individual pursuits for personal gain. Accordingly, when work interferes with family in Singapore (or other collectivistic cultures), it might be accepted as the price to pay for providing for one's family. On the other hand, when work interferes with family in the United States (or other individualistic cultures), it might be viewed as selfish pursuits on the part of the worker that sacrifice the good of his/her loved ones. Considering the depression–conflict link discussed in chapter 2, these results have clear implications for ongoing family conflict processes.

Cultural assumptions underlying WFC are also evident in Lau's (2010) study of fathers' WFC in Hong Kong. Lau found that fathers' work→family conflict was negatively related to the quality of their father–child interactions. Interestingly, mothers' parental involvement functioned as a protective factor, indicating the persistent sex role expectation in dual-earner families. Lau's results call into question the assumption that family members in collectivistic cultures simply accept demanding work as a beneficial sacrifice. Rather, this area is ripe for further studies to unpack the complexities of culture, family, and work as experienced in different family forms across the globe.

One approach for such studies would be to use a family resilience framework to look at the interplay of work–family conflict with work–family facilitation. We discuss this approach in the last section of the chapter. Before we turn to family resilience, however, we discuss another set of family challenges that has garnered significant empirical attention related to family conflict: chronic physical health conditions, mental health issues, and disabilities.

Health, Disability, and Family Conflict

Of all the experiences family members expect to encounter over the lifespan, dealing with chronic illness or with an ongoing disability are among the least expected. However, these challenges do arise in family life. The issue then becomes, not *if* family dynamics will be affected by health and disability issues, but *when* family members will encounter these challenges and *how* they will cope individually and collectively. A considerable amount of research has investigated family interaction processes in the face of these challenges. We cannot possibly review all findings, topics, or research programs in this chapter. What we will do, though, is highlight broad themes regarding health and disability research as they relate to family conflict processes. This research area encompasses a wide array of disciplines, including communication, family studies, sociology, psychology, social work, and oncology, just to name a few.

Physical Health Issues

One interesting conflict concept in the literature on families of children with chronic illnesses is *miscarried helping*. This interaction pattern, most commonly associated with parents and adolescents with chronic health conditions such as diabetes, involves a spiral of caregiving investment, resentment, poor outcomes, and blame (Harris et al., 2008). What starts out as concerned caregiving ends up as conflict. According to Harris et al., this pattern emerges when parents do not consider their adosescent childrens' abilities to make health management decisions, instead making care decisions for their children. This insistence of "parent knows best" can lead to adolescents rebelling and resisting necessary medical treatments. In these cases, we can see that it is not the chronic health problem that "causes" conflict in the family; rather, it is the dynamics of fairly typical parent–adolescent conflicts over autonomy (see chapter 4) magnified by the existence of health issues that require care.

This interaction pattern of care-based conflict is quite serious when considering the importance of managing chronic health conditions. For example, Miller-Johnson et al. (1994) found a consistent association between ratings of parent–child conflict and adherence to diabetes treatment regimens, and symptom control. Although they did not specifically study miscarried helping, results from the Miller-Johnson et al. study clearly revealed that parent–child conflict was a risk factor for diabetes care and control.

All health conditions are not equal, however, when it comes to conflict interactions. For instance, Gerhardt et al. (2003) studied a number of family dynamics, including conflict, in families of children with rheumatoid arthritis compared to families of children without that condition. They found no differences between groups in all areas of family functioning. In another study, Gerhardt and colleagues compared family dynamics between families of children with cancer and families of healthy children (Gerhardt et al., 2007). The only difference between the two groups of families was that mothers of children with cancer reported fewer conflicts than did mothers of children without cancer.

Although Gerhardt et al. (2007) found differences in conflict frequencies between families of children with and without cancer, these findings should be understood within the larger body of research regarding family dynamics in the context of cancer. Quite a bit of research attention has been paid to the impact of cancer on family interactions and relationships. In a literature review of quantitative and qualitative studies concerning the impact of childhood cancer on parents' relationships, da Silva et al. (2010) concluded that research indicates both positive and negative relationship outcomes for parents. For example, one positive outcome reported by parents is an increased ability to resolve conflicts (Lavee & May-Dan, 2003). On the other hand, other studies indicate that parents experience increased role conflict when cancer becomes part of their family experience (e.g., Chesler & Parry, 2001). In a meta-analysis, Pai et al. (2007) also found mixed results when comparing outcomes in families with and without children with cancer. For instance, mothers' reports of family conflict indicate significantly more conflict in families of children with cancer than in families of children without cancer. But there were no significant differences when fathers reported on family conflict. This sex difference might (again) point to how women tend to be more sensitive to relational processes.

Clearly, we should exercise caution when making generalizations about the impact of physical illnesses on family conflict processes. Indeed, Kramer et al. (2009) noted the importance of understanding the variability in family conflict experiences across cancer populations as well as across sources of conflict. A likely difference occurs in family conflict communication when the person with cancer is 5 years old than when the person with cancer is 65 years old, though this is an empirical question that has yet to be addressed. Similarly, different family outcomes likely occur when parents internally experience increased role conflicts than when parents explicitly have conflicts over scheduling demands, financial resources, and the like.

Just as research on work–family conflict has developed over the years to take more nuanced approaches to WFC, research in the area of cancer and other physical health conditions clearly points to the need to take a more nuanced approach to family conflict processes. Researchers need to move beyond comparing frequencies between families with and without cancer to identifying specific conflict topics, tactics, and outcomes associated with different conflict processes. Such an approach to processes and outcomes might yield pathways for guiding families to productive conflict interactions as they face chronic physical health conditions across the lifespan.

Mental Health Issues

The mental health of family members also influences ways in which members engage in conflict and experience outcomes of that conflict. As indicated in chapter 2, a cyclical connection exists between conflict communication and depression. Studies have clearly linked mothers' and fathers' clinical depression with parent–child conflict, marital conflict, parental problem drinking, and child behavioral problems (Du Rocher Schudlich &

Cummings, 2007; El-Sheikh & Flanagan, 2001; Kane & Garber, 2004; Shelton & Harold, 2008).

An important set of findings that emerges across studies is the role that family conflict plays in the link between parental depression and child outcomes. Studies focusing on various stages of the family life cycle, from when children are toddlers (Caughy et al., 2009) to when they are in elementary school (El-Sheikh & Flanagan, 2001) to when they are adolescents (Du Rocher Schudlich & Cummings, 2007), indicate that marital conflict and parent–child conflict link parental depressive symptoms and various child outcomes, including mother–child attachment (Caughy et al., 2009), emotional security (Du Rocher Schudlich & Cummings, 2007), internalizing, externalizing, and social problems (El-Sheikh & Flanagan, 2001; Fear et al., 2009).

For example, Caughy et al. (2009) studied mother–toddler dyads in structured play sessions in a laboratory and again in unstructured play sessions in homes. Results indicated both quantitative and qualitative differences in mother–toddler conflict interactions, specifically in the structured setting. More conflict occurred in dyads with depressed mothers and depressed mothers were more likely to respond to their toddlers in destructive ways (such as scolding, threatening, etc.). However, non-depressed mothers were more likely to give in to their children. Interestingly, although this study found that these conflict interactions linked maternal depression and mother–child attachment, mother–toddler conflict did not filter the association between early depression in mothers and later problem behaviors in children (Caughy et al., 2009, p. 16).

As children get older, family conflict seems to play a larger role in the association between parental depression and child outcomes, such as internalizing (depressive symptoms), externalizing (acting out inappropriately or aggressively), and other social interaction/development problems. Marital conflict interactions and parent–child conflict interactions have emerged as filters between parental depression and these important child outcomes. For example, Shelton and Harold (2008) conducted a longitudinal study to investigate associations between parental depression, marital conflict, and parent–child relationship quality. Results of that study indicate that interparental conflict at one point in time was significantly related to adolescents' perceptions that their mothers and fathers rejected rather than accepted them. In fact, this study over time was able to show how parental depression at an earlier point in time was related to more marital conflict at a later time, which in turn was related to adolescents' reports of being rejected by their parents a year later. Furthermore, results indicated that parent–child rejection was significantly related to both internalizing and externalizing problems for adolescents.

Research attempting to understand complex associations between family member conditions (such as depression) and behavior (such as problem drinking or aggressiveness) frequently reflects the systems perspective on families (chapter 1). This perspective is very useful for explaining ways in which family members influence each other and for demonstrating the impact of interactions throughout family life. For example, Du Rocher Schudlich and Cummings (2007) used emotional security theory (see chapter 3), which is grounded in the systems perspective, to frame their study of parental depression, marital conflict, and child adjustment problems. These researchers found that the association between parental depression and child adjustment problems was connected by depressive marital conflict (e.g., withdrawal, sadness, fear). Additionally, results of this study indicate that mothers' and fathers' depression were negatively related to constructive marital conflict tactics (e.g., humor, physical affection, problem solving) and positively related to depressive and destructive marital conflict tactics (e.g., hostility, defensiveness). In terms of emotional security, depressive conflict was negatively related to children's emotional security, while constructive conflict and child emotional security were negatively related to child adjustment problems. Similarly, El-Sheikh and Flanagan (2001) used the emotional regulation framework to interpret results of their study concerning parental depression, problem drinking, and children's behavior problems. The emotional regulation framework holds that family conflict influences children's emotionality and regulation of those emotions, which can lead to problem behavior. Their study found that marital and parent–child conflict filtered the association between parents' problem drinking and children's internalizing, externalizing, and social problems. These studies demonstrate ways in which parental conditions, such as depression, and interaction behavior, such as conflict tactics, impact children's emotional development and adjustment as well as children's behavior.

Of course, parents are not the only family members whose mental health affects family conflict processes. Marmorstein and Iacono (2004) studied conflict in families with adolescents who had either major depression or conduct disorder. Not surprisingly, they found that adolescents with either of these conditions had more conflict with both mothers and fathers. However, families that also included depressed mothers had even more mother–child conflict.

Similarly, research regarding eating disorders reveals that disordered eating by children at an earlier point in time was related to higher parent–child conflict a full three years later (Spanos et al., 2010). The authors noted that common knowledge, including among clinicians, places family conflict as a potential "cause" of eating disorders. However, results of this study demonstrate the opposite mechanism occurring – the eating disorder led to higher family conflict. This study, over a six-year period of time, demonstrates the value of longitudinal studies for understanding the interdependence of family member conditions and behaviors over time.

As with other family conflict processes, family experiences of health and disability are shaped by broader sociocultural contexts. Ma (2005, 2008) examined ways in which traditional Chinese cultural assumptions about family roles and conflict are manifest in families of women with eating disorders. Consistent with findings in the Spanos et al. (2010) study, Ma found that most family conflicts identified were results of, rather than contributing factors of, eating disorders of one of the family members. Furthermore, Ma found a tendency for family members to avoid conflicts outside of a clinical context, which she noted reflects a cultural value of maintaining family harmony (Ma, 2005, p. 38). She also argued that parent–child conflict often concerns issues of power and control between generations in a rapidly changing society. Ma's studies reinforce our assertions throughout this book that family conflict researchers need to attend to cultural contexts when investigating various aspects of family conflict communication.

Disabilities

It is important to recognize that not all physical and mental challenges facing families will involve illness *per se*. Family members often have disabilities, visible or invisible, that influence family dynamics in general and conflict interactions specifically. Disabilities are not illnesses. Rather, they are physical, mental, and/or emotional conditions that affect family life. Many times people with disabilities also have, or develop, health problems. For example, a child who cannot walk and has other physical issues due to the birth defect of spina bifida is not "sick." Rather, spina bifida is a physical life condition for that child and his or her family. Children with this disability often undergo surgeries to lessen the severity of their symptoms, and frequently this birth defect includes health problems. In such cases a connection exists between disability issues and health issues. Much has been written in the disability literature about removing the dichotomy of ability–disability from our language and refraining from thinking of people with disabilities as "sick." We will not go into detail about that debate here (see Canary, 2008b for review of this issue). We wish to simply note that people with disabilities are able to do some things, not able to do others, and their conditions are not illnesses that can be "cured" with medical attention. Research of families with people with disabilities indicates that the nature and severity of a disability affects how the presence of disability impacts families in different ways (Canary, 2008a; Stoneman, 2001). For this reason we discuss separately "visible" disabilities, such as spina bifida, and "invisible" disabilities, such as attention deficit/hyperactivity disorder (ADHD).

Visible disabilities

Interestingly, not as much research exists as one would think regarding conflict processes in families of people with visible disabilities. There could be a number of reasons for the lack of research in this context. First, it is very difficult to recruit participants, particularly multiple family members, from this population. Families are busy. Families managing issues such as mobility impairment have added burdens of scheduling appointments with professional support providers and transporting family members to those appointments. Taking time to participate in research studies is burdensome and intrusive. Another reason for a lack of research in this area is that for some disabilities, such as deafness and blindness, there is likely very little difference in conflict processes between this population and the broader family population.

Research comparing families with members who have a disability to families without disabilities is mixed in terms of conflict processes. For example, Nixon and Cummings (1999) combined visible and invisible disabilities in their study of siblings of children with disabilities. Compared to siblings of children without disabilities, siblings of children with disabilities in that study "assumed more responsibility, expected more involvement, and perceived more threat in response to all types of conflict situations" (Nixon & Cummings, 1999, p. 281). Importantly, this study was an experiment that showed conflict scenes to children to gauge their responses to conflict that reflected typical interparental, sibling, and peer conflict. These researchers explained, using emotional security theory, that children who are exposed to more stress and conflict in everyday family life will be more sensitized to conflict and have a lower response threshold. Results were interpreted from the perspective that the context of disability, whether visible or invisible, increases overall family stress and therefore children are more sensitive to conflict in the family.

When looking at the actual amount of conflict in families with and without disabilities, however, results are different. One group of researchers expected families of children with spina bifida to have different levels of conflict and cohesion than families of children without the condition (Coakley et al., 2002; Jandasek et al.,

2009). They were most interested in changes over time as children with and without spina bifida experience puberty and enter the highly conflictual adolescent stage. They found that families with a child with spina bifida experienced less conflict and more cohesion as children entered adolescence, whereas families without spina bifida experienced more conflict and less cohesion during that transitional time. One interpretation of these results is that children with spina bifida experience puberty in a less dramatic way than adolescents without the condition, and parents might be in denial about the maturation of their children with spina bifida (Coakley et al., 2002). However, that interpretation does not explain the increased cohesion reported in families with spina bifida. The researchers later noted that these results offer some support for a disruption-resilience model that indicates families develop areas of strength and vulnerability when they experience chronic illness (Jandasek et al., 2009, p. 736). Particularly due to the increased cohesion found in families with spina bifida, we will return to this idea later in the chapter when we discuss family resilience as a productive approach for family conflict research.

Invisible disabilities
Invisible disabilities are not evident simply by observing a person casually. These disabilities occur across the lifespan and include seizure disorders, learning disabilities, autism spectrum disorders, and dementia. Invisible disabilities can be more confusing for family members to deal with because of their multiple manifestations and often changing symptoms (Canary, 2008b). Research indicates that there might be a bi-directional relationship between invisible disabilities and family conflict. Differing results across studies likely is due to different life stages of participating families (i.e., early childhood, adolescent children, or elderly family members) as well as varying degrees of severity and differing symptoms across disabilities.

For instance, Kelly et al. (2008) investigated associations among family conflict, child anxiety and depression, and autism spectrum disorder (ASD) symptoms. This study of families with young children found that greater levels of family conflict were associated with more anxiety and depression in children, which in turn pre-dicted the presence of ASD symptoms (p. 1077). The researchers tested for the opposite path as well, that ASD symptoms would lead to more family conflict and association, but that was not supported. Accordingly, although the Kelly et al. study was cross-sectional, their results call into question the assumption often underlying, if not explicitly stated in, research that the presence of disability in a family creates a stressful context that is detrimen-tal to family dynamics (Nixon & Cummings, 1999). Similarly, Scharlach et al. (2006) found that the impact of elderly care recipi-ents' severity of mental impairment on caregiver (usually family members) outcomes was fully mediated by family conflict. Thus, as with other health and disability issues discussed thus far, it is not the existence of a condition that causes negative outcomes as much as the family conflict nested within that context that can lead to negative outcomes for family members.

Research regarding attention deficit hyperactivity disorder (ADHD) provides exceptions to this general conclusion, although results across studies are not consistent. ADHD is a disability primarily affecting attention and impulsivity management, often leading to inappropriate interaction behavior (Edwards et al., 2001). People with ADHD often have other conditions that affect their behavior and social interactions as well, including mood disorders and substance abuse (Lee et al., 2011). Research indi-cates that the presence of ADHD in a family can influence conflict interactions. Yet a direct association was called into question by a study of families of children with ADHD that found mothers' level of distress (anxiety, depression, and hostility) connected the rela-tionship between children's behavior problems and family conflict (Kendall et al., 2005). However, Wymbs and Palham, Jr. (2010) studied potential effects of children with ADHD on their parents' interactions. The experimental study used children as confeder-ates who behaved either as if they had ADHD or did not have the condition. Participants engaged in dyadic discussions about how to handle children's behavior, observers coded their interaction behavior as positive or negative, and then participants rated their partners' coparenting discussion behavior as positive or negative.

Comparisons between parents of children with ADHD, parents of children with ADHD and oppositional defiance disorder (ODD) or conduct disorder (CD), and parents with children without a disability diagnosis indicated that parents of children with multiple diagnoses rated their partners' coparenting interactions less positively when dealing with a disruptive child than did participants in the other two groups. Likewise, observers rated parents of both clinical groups as more negative when interacting in the disruptive child condition than parents without a diagnosed child.

Other studies have examined ways in which children with ADHD and other co-existing conditions interact with family members. For instance, Mikami and Pfiffner (2008) studied sibling conflict when one sibling had both ADHD and externalizing behavior problems. Sibling pairs in that study had more conflict when both conditions were present than when they were not present. Due to impaired self-control involved with ADHD, these result are not surprising. Similarly, Edwards et al. (2001) found an impact on parent–child conflict when adolescents had both ADHD and ODD. Comparing these families to a community sample without ADHD or ODD, parents and adolescents reported more conflict issues, greater anger intensity during conflicts, and more aggressive conflict tactics than the community comparison group. This research group used coercion theory to interpret results, concluding that families develop more aggressive and coercive tactics over time as they interact with each other and reinforce the use of aggression. On the other hand, families might also reinforce more constructive interactional tactics over time, regardless of the presence of disability or not. In the following section, we discuss how a family resilience approach offers promise for studies of family conflict in the face of challenges.

Family Resilience and Conflict

Throughout this book we have attempted to draw a picture of the consequentiality of family conflict. Although the topic has garnered significant empirical attention across a number of disciplines, much of that research reflects a negative bias regarding conflict in families (e.g., chapter 3). That is, general measures of conflict levels are examined for connections to negative outcomes for individual family members as well as for family systems as a whole (e.g., Shelton & Harold, 2008). Some research provides a more sophisticated view of the multiple ways conflict functions in families by tapping constructive conflict interactions as well as destructive conflict interactions (e.g., Caughy et al., 2009). We close this book by focusing on a positive approach for studying conflict interactions in families. This is our opportunity to connect with the recent cross-disciplinary interest in family resiliency.

McCubbin and McCubbin led the way in developing a theoretical model of family resiliency in the early 1990s (McCubbin & McCubbin, 1993). Empirical attention to the topic in the communication discipline has only emerged since the turn of the century (e.g., Golish, 2003). We focus on the promise this approach holds for studies of family conflict.

What is family resilience? Several definitions have been offered (e.g., Marsh et al., 1996; McCubbin & McCubbin, 1996). They all recognize that family resilience constitutes abilities of family systems and their individual members to use resources (internal and external) as strengths to adapt to stressors and crises that occur over the lifespan. Some researchers use the terms *family strengths* or *strong families* rather than the term *resilience*, but these terms mean essentially the same thing. McCubbin and McCubbin's early theoretical work provides the following definition of family resiliency:

> the positive behavioral patterns and functional competencies individuals and the family unit demonstrate under stressful or adverse circumstances, which determine the family's ability to recover by maintaining its integrity as a unit while insuring, and where necessary restoring, the well-being of family members and the family unit as a whole. (McCubbin & McCubbin, 1996, p. 5)

In her International Communication Association presidential address, Patrice Buzzanell (2010) noted the importance of having a process view of resilience – that it is ongoing and dynamic, developing over time. She further conjectured that five processes form resiliency: crafting normalcy, affirming foundations of one's identity, maintaining and using communication networks, putting alternative logics to work, and legitimizing negative feelings while foregrounding productive action (p. 3). What are connections between family resiliency and family conflict communication? We discuss what research reveals about these connections and offer suggestions for future studies taking a resiliency approach to family conflict.

Clearly, family conflict processes either contribute to or detract from the development of family strengths and resiliency (Cook & DeFrain, 2005; Schrodt, 2009). In general terms, Schrodt found an inverse relationship between conflict avoidance and family strength. That is, families that tend to "avoid conflict either by suppressing unpleasant topics or by enforcing conformity to family rules" also tend to have fewer strengths as a unit (p. 181). Again using broad strokes, Cook and DeFrain concluded in their study of families that strong families (who we would also call resilient families) tended to use positive communication, including "talking to clear the air" as a tactic for conflict management (2005, p. 8). Black and Lobo (2008) identified several factors characteristic of resilient families: a positive outlook, spirituality, family member accord, flexibility, communication, financial management, time together, mutual recreational interests, routines and rituals, and social support (p. 37). Although not all of these factors concern conflict processes, several of them point to strategies and tactics associated with constructive conflict management processes (chapters 2, 3, 4, and 5). Because we know that conflict is inevitable in families over the lifespan, including when family members face stressors and crises, these general findings indicate that the mere presence of conflict is less predictive of family resilience (or not) than is the interactive strategies family members use to manage conflicts that arise.

To return to themes discussed in previous chapters, research findings regarding romantic partner conflict, parent–child, and sibling conflict point to ways in which conflict interaction can build family strengths or capabilities and lead to more adaptive, resilient family units. For example, our discussion in chapter 4 about conflict processes and outcomes highlighted positive child outcomes related to constructive conflict interaction tactics used in parent–child conflict across the family lifespan. Over time, conflict interactions between parents and children that involve compromise, reasoning, and problem solving lead to family members who display prosocial behaviors, construct healthy self-identities, and maintain quality relationships with other members (see tables 4.1–4.3). These outcomes directly map onto processes and characteristics of resiliency and family resilience, such as positive communication, commitment (Cook & DeFrain, 2005), flexibility, and collaboration (Black & Lobo, 2008).

Research concerning family resilience has often been conducted in contexts of challenges discussed earlier in this chapter, the work–family interface, health, and disability (Maguire, 2012). For example, Grzywacz and Bass (2003) used a family resilience framework to examine how family members experience both work–family conflict and work–family facilitation. Work–family facilitation "represents the synergies or complementarities that occur when individuals combine work and family" (Grzywacz & Bass, p. 249). For example, Dan and Heather find connections between their family interactions, movies they watch together, other research they conduct, and the process of writing this book. The results of the Grzywacz and Bass study indicate that "work–family facilitation, as a family capability, may help families adjust to work–family conflict by offsetting or redefining the meaning of the incoming stressor, thereby eliminating its threat" (p. 255). Here we see ways in which using roles, skills, and attitudes from the family domain constitute a family strength that help members and the unit as a whole adapt to the inevitable role conflict associated with functioning in work and family systems.

Likewise, research discussed in the previous sections regarding health and disability point to ways in which the mere presence of a chronic health condition or disability does not necessarily lead to poorer outcomes for families. Rather, how family members manage their interpersonal conflicts often connects health/disability to well-being indicators. More work should follow models such as the Du Rocher Schudlich and Cummings (2007) study, with research designs that tap different conflict management tactics used in the context of chronic health and disability issues to unpack ways in which conflict may contribute to family resilience or detract from it. Global measures of conflict presence or frequency are less useful when developing interventions for families who want (and need) to increase their capacities for adapting to stress and change as they face health and disability over the lifespan.

Implications

We opened this chapter by noting that many common family challenges are unexpected, such as feeling caught between work and family, dealing with a life-threatening illness of a family member, or handling a chronic disability. However, as numerous family researchers and counselors will attest, families should expect to encounter challenges and should expect that such stressful situations will influence their family interactions in varied ways (Maguire, 2012).

Perhaps predictably, conflicts between work roles/obligations and family roles/obligations spill over into family interactions and relationship qualities. Although it might not be realistic to expect to eliminate such conflicts, family members can manage this challenge by drawing on constructive conflict management tactics such as negotiation and compromise, direct communication, and expressing positivity. Another way to manage the work–family interface is to find ways to create work–family facilitation, which includes re-framing the interface so family members might benefit from synergies of work and family life. This might involve some creative problem solving on the part of family members, which in turn contributes to family resilience.

Nobody wants to anticipate poor health and disability as part of family experiences, but it is realistic to do so. When chronic health and disability conditions are part of everyday family life, stresses and strains inevitably impact interactions. However, research is also clear that the mere existence of illness or disability is far less influential to family relationships than the communication behaviors family members choose to use when interacting with each other, including during conflicts. The research is quite clear that *how* we treat each other during disagreements is much more important for family outcomes and functioning than is the presence of health problems or disabilities. In contexts of health problems and disability, family members have many opportunities to express affection, develop cohesion, and creatively problem solve as they encounter conflicts and difficulties. These behaviors are signs of resilience, but they are also processes that *build* resilient families.

Final Thoughts on Family Conflict

This book concerned family conflict – its nature and processes. Each chapter both described the nature of the relationship being examined and how conflict management processes are portrayed in the research. At the heart of this book lies one persistent fact: how families manage conflict represents a critically important process. Family conflicts affect each person in the family, in terms of their emotional states and individual well-being. Family conflicts also affect the relationships between and among family members perhaps more strongly than other interaction behaviors. Family relationships become more unstable to the extent conflicts are managed poorly, but they gain momentum to the extent conflicts are managed productively though constructive communication strategies and tactics. This book also identified implications based on the research literature. Hundreds of studies point to nonintuitive or little-known findings that might surprise the reader. Although the empirical research on family conflict provides a broad and deep pool of knowledge, we envision future possibilities. First, we hope that researchers focus more on constructive communication processes. As the reader has discovered, much of the research has emphasized negative features of conflict, such as its ongoing frequency, intensity, and aggression (for example, in chapter 3 on interparental conflict; chapter 5 on adolescent sibling conflict). The portrayal of family conflict as inherently negative misses the positive functional possibilities of conflict management (Putnam, 2006). For instance, we know that constructive communicative strategies lead to greater relational satisfaction, family cohesion, marital stability, and perceived warmth between siblings.

Second, we need richer descriptions of family conflict processes, a point that applies both to negative and positive dimensions of conflict messages. The research on marital interaction sequences and research involving early childhood participants provide some exellent descriptions of family conflict processes. We hope that similar inroads could be made elsewhere. An excellent research strategy, used by many cited in this book, would involve complementing survey approaches with observational analyses. Although questionnaires are valuable for assessing perceptions, they are a step removed from actual interaction. To obtain a rich understanding of family conflict processes, one finds representations of interaction as it unfolds, continues, and terminates.

We find the family resilience framework to offer tremendous promise for future studies of family conflict. A great need remains for basic communication research to connect to applied contexts of family interventions. Conflict can be very difficult. Conflict is pervasive. Conflict can tear family members apart. Conflict can help individual family members construct healthy self-identities and non-family relationships. Conflict can move family systems to new levels of functionality. All of these represent reasons to continue to investigate connections between family conflict and the development of resilient families. We encourage readers to do so.

Appendix 1

Discussion Questions

Chapter 1: Introduction to Family Conflict

1. Several reasons were offered to study family conflict. Can you think of additional reasons, based on your own knowledge or personal experience? Please elaborate on your answer. If you cannot think of additional reasons, then which of those offered is the most compelling to you? Why?

2. What do you think of the authors' definition of *family conflict?* Is each term adequately represented – that is, "family" and "conflict"? Does the authors' definition of "family conflict" support or differ from your own understanding of conflict that occurs in families? Please elaborate.

3. Koerner and Fitzpatrick's family typology shows that families manage conflict differently. One potential problem arises if one family member does not accept the definition of the family that the others adopt. What kinds of conflicts might erupt due to different expectations about what the family should resemble? How might conflict messages differ among the parties to this conflict?

4. Three different theoretic approaches were covered in chapter 1. What is the usefulness in presenting these theories? Which of these theoretic approaches provides you the most information for studying family conflict? Please elaborate on your answer.

5. Toward the end of the chapter, the authors present a multi-level model of family conflict (see fig. 1.2). Do you concur with

the organization of the model – that individual experiences lie at the center of the model, and cultural factors surround the other features of the model? Please elaborate. If you were to represent family conflict processes, would you rely on this model? Please explain.

Chapter 2: Marital Conflict

1. Some people manage conflict similar to how their parents managed conflict. Other people make adjustments and might even behave in ways opposite to their parents. Do you tend to behave like your parents in terms of your conflicts? What specific conflict tactics do you use that they did? Or what specific conflict tactics do you use that they did not?

2. As noted in chapter 2, marriages come in different forms, or types. Each of these is satisfactory if partners buy into the same type of marriage. Which of these (Traditional, Independent, Separate) is the most desirable type in your view? If in a romantic relationship, do you and your partner value the same type? How do your conflict behaviors reflect the type of relationship you have? If not in a romantic involvement, what type of partner might you want?

3. Look at the negative and positive conflict sequences in tables 2.2 and 2.3. These sequences show how two partners' conflict messages combine. Which negative sequence(s) do you find yourself falling into? Which positive sequence(s) do you engage in? Can you think of other sequences that two people jointly create? Please offer examples for your answers.

4. Do you find that intense and negative conflict interactions increase your level of depression? If so, how does that happen specifically – for example, when do you feel your depression increase? If not, what other emotional reactions do you have to negative conflict interactions? Anger? Sadness? Nervousness? Relief?

5. Gottman's model of divorce highlights the role of conflict communication and how people react to it. Think of the divorce process between two people you know. Did it follow the specific

paths that Gottman's model indicates? Or did it follow different paths? Please explain.

Chapter 3: Interparental Conflict, Post-Divorce, and Stepfamilies

1. Interparental conflict (IPC) can powerfully affect children's internal and external adjustment problems. Also, IPC can spill over into the parent–child relationship. Have you or a friend ever experienced a spillover event, where the parents' conflict(s) affected the relationship with a parent? What conflict behaviors did the parents use? What was the spillover effect? That is, what aspect of the parent–child relationship was negatively affected?

2. Feeling caught in the middle is one of the most troubling, difficult experiences a child can have. Ironically, the research shows that parents who engage in triangulation attempts are seen as less competent and satisfactory. Have you or someone you know ever been caught in the middle of the parents' argument(s)? How did you or your friend respond?

3. Do you believe that emotional security theory applies to people who are over 15 years old? If so, what is the emotional security dependent on? If not, then what other processes become important when viewing the relevance of IPC for the adolescent or young adult?

4. Divorce and conflict affect the child and his or her future relationships. Do you agree that staying in a high-conflict home is worse for the child than having the parents divorce? Why? Do you know anyone who comes from a divorced home? What are their typical conflict strategies? Do you think these conflict behaviors stem from his or her broken home? What are the prospects for their commitment to a future partner? Please elaborate.

5. Note the climate of the stepfamily indicates what conflict issues they face and how they manage conflict. Do you know someone who has a dysfunctional stepfamily? In what ways is it dysfunctional? What conflict issues do the family members face? How

do they manage those conflicts? Contrast these conflict behaviors with a functional stepfamily that you know.

Chapter 4: Conflict between Parents and Children

1. What role does theory play in increasing understanding of parent–child conflict? Are there theories not represented in this chapter that would be useful for framing future studies of parent–child conflict? If so, what are they?
2. The two main age cohorts represented in parent–child conflict research are toddlers/preschoolers and adolescents. Why is this the case? What might you take from research of these two age groups and apply to elementary-aged children? What types of topics, processes, and outcomes might you focus on for children aged 5–10?
3. Another under-represented age cohort for understanding parent–child conflict is adult children. With the aging population across the globe, what types of topics, processes, and outcomes might we focus on in future studies? From your own experience, does this type of conflict matter? Why or why not?
4. Single parents face many challenges regarding work–life conflict. Single parents often lack the resources to raise their children, and their conflicts tend to be more negative than those in dual-parent homes. What advice for managing parent–child conflict would you give to a single parent? Please elaborate.
5. What is your reaction to conclusions that studies of middle-class European Americans do not always generalize to other cultural populations? What can researchers do to better understand cultural differences in parent–child conflict processes?

Chapter 5: Siblings in Conflict

1. We offer several insights that parents might use to take constructive approaches to sibling conflicts in early childhood. How do these parental involvement suggestions relate to your own experiences from childhood or to your own experiences as

a parent? What are some specific tactics parents might use to increase constructive sibling conflicts and decrease destructive sibling conflicts in early childhood?

2. What might adult siblings argue about? We discussed how processes and outcomes of childhood sibling conflict are carried into adolescence. In what ways do you think adolescent sibling conflict is (or is not) carried into adulthood?

3. Approximately 60 percent of adolescent conflicts are managed in a destructive way, for example, through aggression. Does the amount of aggression in adolescent sibling conflicts surprise you? What precautions can a parent take to minimize the amount of adolescent sibling conflict, based on the ideas offered in chapter 5?

4. The sex composition of siblings appears to affect how conflict is managed. In your experience (either your family or someone else's), do opposite-sex siblings have more or less contentious conflicts than same-sex siblings? Or is there no difference? Please offer examples and an explanation for your answer.

5. This chapter does not offer much in the way of cultural influences on sibling conflict. Based on your own experiences and on what you have read about cultural influences on family conflict in general, what do you think might be similarities and differences in sibling conflict across cultures? What are some experiences that lead to these suggestions?

Chapter 6: Conflict in the Face of Family Challenges

1. This chapter discusses ways the work–family interface influences, and is influenced by, family conflict processes. How do issues and findings discussed in this chapter relate to your own experiences of managing your personal life and professional life? How have you experienced these tensions?

2. What gaps or future directions do you see for studying the impact of physical and/or mental health on family conflict processes? What theories or methods do you see as useful for

expanding our understanding of this important area?

3. Focusing on disabilities as they relate to family conflict could be seen as viewing disabilities as inherently difficult or stressful for family processes. How might we continue to study conflict processes in families of people with disabilities without taking a deficit approach to disabilities?

4. Discuss the role of family resiliency in conflict processes. How can you incorporate strategies and perspectives associated with resilience to improve your own family conflict processes as you encounter unexpected events throughout your lifespan?

Appendix 2

Family Conflict at the Movies

Chapter 1: Introduction to Family Conflict

The Family Stone (2005, PG-13) is a comedy about changes a family goes through as members grow up, have children, introduce new members, and more. An all-star cast including Diane Keaton, Sarah Jessica Parker, and Luke Wilson provide a poignant mix of comedy and drama. This is an excellent example of the interdependence of family subsystems and the inevitability of family conflict processes.

Chapter 2: Marital Conflict

American Beauty (1999, R), starring Kevin Spacey and Annette Benning, shows how one married couple do not face up to their lack of intimacy. The husband, whose mid-life crisis is palpable, confronts the wife. But she ignores his advances and shows dismay at his life change.

Who's Afraid of Virginia Woolf? (1966, NR) presents the dark side of marriage built on fantasy. It stars Elizabeth Taylor and Richard Burton, who play Martha and George. They throw an impromptu party where they publically demonstrate their intolerance for each other. Sarcasm, contempt, ridicule, and indirect complaints salt the dialogue.

The Lion in Winter (1968, NR) is replete with various negative and positive communication behaviors. The problem concerns how the negative well outweighs the positive, and the interparental conflict spills over into their relationships with their children.

Crazy, Stupid Love (2011, PG-13) examines how one man copes with marital separation, while trying to maintain his relationship with his children. This comedy, starring Steve Carrell, Ryan Gosling, and Julianne Moore, shows how the husband adjusts to separation by taking on a new life. But the most poignant scene occurs when he moves out but cannot communicate with his wife, who wants to discuss their marital problems at a most inconvenient time.

Chapter 3: Interparental Conflict, Post-Divorce, and Stepfamilies

The Santa Clause (1994, PG) stars Tim Allen in this fantasy comedy about a divorced father and his son. It includes several examples of interparental and post-divorce conflict.

Yours, Mine, and Ours (2005, PG), starring Rene Russo and Dennis Quaid, is about a stepfamily created when a widower with 10 children marries a widow with 7 children. The movie is replete with examples of stepfamily conflict.

Kramer vs. Kramer (1979, PG) stars Dustin Hoffman and Meryl Streep. This movie recounts the divorce process between Hoffman and Streep and the ensuing custody battle as Hoffman tries to retain custody of their son.

Chapter 4: Conflict between Parents and Children

Good Deeds (2012, PG-13) introduces us to a single mother who is struggling to make ends meet while raising her six-year-old daughter. This film does a nice job of presenting a single mother's plight, the responsibility she places on her daughter, and how they manage conflicts. The film stars Thandie Newton as the single mother, along with Tyler Perry and Gabrielle Union.

The Perfect Family (2011, PG-13) delves into conflict between a mother and her adult children. Featuring Kathleen Turner and Emily Deschanel, this story also highlights ways that marital tensions spill over into parent–child relationships.

October Sky (1999, PG), starring Jake Gyllenhaal and Laura Dern, is based on the true story of a boy who wanted to leave his small mining town to become a rocket scientist. His father had other ideas for his future, providing many scenes of father–adolescent son conflict.

Chapter 5: Siblings in Conflict

The Brothers Bloom (2008, PG-13), starring Adrien Brody and Mark Ruffalo, follows two brothers through their antics as con men. The sibling conflict is mostly covert but emerges overtly in select scenes.

Chapter 6: Conflict in the Face of Family Challenges

My Sister's Keeper (2009, PG-13) introduces several conflicts as a family goes through the cancer journey of one of the children. The primary conflict is between one of the daughters, Anna, and her parents, as she seeks medical emancipation from them in court. However, the movie highlights how cancer is a family experience and can impact conflict processes throughout the family.

Ordinary People (1980, R) tells the painful story of a family rocked by the untimely death of one of the sons. The movie, starring Donald Sutherland and Mary Tyler Moore as the parents, points to the interdependence of family relationships and experiences that influence how conflicts are managed in the family following a tragedy.

References

Ackerman, R. A., Kashy, D. A., Donnellan, M. B. & Conger, R. D. (2011). Positive-engagement behaviors in observed family interactions: A social relations perspective. *Journal of Family Psychology, 25*, 719–30.

Adams, R. E. & Laursen, B. (2001). The organization and dynamics of adolescent conflict with parents and friends. *Journal of Marriage and Family, 63*, 97–110.

Adams, R. E. & Laursen, B. (2007). The correlates of conflict: Disagreement is not necessarily detrimental. *Journal of Family Psychology, 21*, 445–58.

Afifi, T. D. (2003). "Feeling caught" in stepfamilies: Managing boundary turbulence through appropriate communication privacy rules. *Journal of Social and Personal Relationships, 20*, 729–55.

Afifi, T. D. & Schrodt, P. (2003a). "Feeling caught" as a mediator of adolescents' and young adults' avoidance and satisfaction with their parents in divorced and non-divorced households. *Communication Monographs, 70*, 142–73.

Afifi, T. D. & Schrodt, P. (2003b). Uncertainty and the avoidance of the state of one's family in stepfamilies, postdivorce, single-parent families, and first-marriage families. *Human Communication Research, 29*, 516–32.

Afifi, T. D., Aldeis, D. & Joseph, A. (2010). Family conflict. In W. R. Cupach, D. J. Canary & B. H. Spitzberg (Eds.), *Competence in interpersonal conflict* (pp. 191–209). Long Grove, IL: Waveland Press.

Ahn, A. J., Kim, B. S. & Park, Y. S. (2009). Asian cultural values gap, cognitive flexibility, coping strategies, and parent–child conflicts among Korean Americans. *Asian American Journal of Psychology, S(1)*, 29–44.

Alexander, J. F. (1973). Defensive and supportive communications in normal and deviant families. *Journal of Consulting and Clinical Psychology, 40*, 223–31.

Allison, B. N. & Schultz, J. B. (2004). Parent–adolescent conflict in early adolescence. *Adolescence, 39*, 101–19.

Amato, P. R. (2001). Children of divorce in the 1990s: An update of the Amato and Keith (1991) meta-analysis. *Journal of Family Psychology, 15*, 355–70.

References

Amato, P. R. (1994). The implications of research findings on children in step-families. In A. Booth & J. Dunn (Eds.), *Stepfamilies: Who benefits? Who does not?* (pp. 81–7). Hillsdale, NJ: Lawrence Erlbaum.

Amato, P. R. & Afifi, T. D. (2006). Feeling caught between parents: Adult children's relations with parents and subjective well-being. *Journal of Marriage and the Family, 68,* 222–35.

Amato, P. R. & DeBoer, D. D. (2001). The transmission of marital instability across generations: Relationship skills or commitment to marriage? *Journal of Marriage and the Family, 63,* 1038–51.

Amato, P. R. & Keith, B. (1991). Parental divorce and the well-being of children: A meta-analysis. *Psychological Bulletin, 110,* 26–46.

Atkinson, E. R., Dadds, M. R., Chipuer, H. & Dawe, S. (2009). Threat is a multidimensional construct: Exploring the role of children's threat appraisals in the relationship between interparental conflict and child adjustment. *Journal of Abnormal Child Psychology, 37,* 281–92.

Avtgis, T. A. (2002). Adult–child conflict control expectancies: Effects on taking conflict personally toward parents. *Communication Research Reports, 19,* 226–36.

Avtgis, T. A. (2003). Male sibling and emotional support as a function of attributional confidence. *Communication Research Reports, 20,* 341–7.

Bank, L., Burraston, B. & Snyder, J. (2004). Sibling conflict and ineffective parenting as predictors of adolescent boys' antisocial behavior and peer difficulties: Additive and interaction effects. *Journal of Research on Adolescence, 14,* 99–125.

Barber, J. G. & Delfabbro, P. (2000). Predictors of adolescent adjustment: Parent–peer relationships and parent–child conflict. *Child and Adolescent Social Work Journal, 17,* 275–88.

Bateson, G. (1951). Information and codification: A philosophical approach. In J. Ruesch & G. Bateson (Eds.), *Communication: The social matrix of psychiatry* (pp. 168–211). New York: Norton.

Baxter, L. A. & Braithwaite, D. O. (2006). Introduction: Meta-theory and theory in family communication research. In D. O. Braithwaite & L. A. Baxter (Eds.), *Engaging theories in family communication* (pp. 1–15). Thousand Oaks, CA: Sage.

Baxter, L. A. & Montgomery, B. M. (1996). *Relating: Dialogues and dialectics.* New York: Guilford.

Baxter, L. A., Braithwaite, D. O., Bryant, L. & Wagner, A. (2004). Stepchildren's perceptions of the contradictions in communication with stepparents. *Journal of Social and Personal Relationships. 21,* 447–67.

Benson, M., Buehler, C. & Gerard, J. M. (2008). Interparental hostility and early adolescent problem behavior: Spillover via maternal acceptance, harshness, inconsistency, and intrusiveness. *The Journal of Early Adolescence, 28,* 428–54.

References

Bermúdez, J. M. & Stinson, M. A. (2011). Redefining conflict resolution styles for Latino couples: Examining the role of gender and culture. *Journal of Feminist Family Therapy, 23*, 71–87.

Birditt, K. S., Rott, L. M. & Fingerman, K. L. (2009). "If you can't say something nice, don't say anything at all": Coping with interpersonal tensions in the parent–child relationship during adulthood. *Journal of Family Psychology, 23*, 769–78.

Birditt, K. S., Brown, E., Orbuch, T. L. & McIlvane, J. M. (2010). Marital conflict behaviors and implications for divorce over 16 years. *Journal of Marriage and the Family, 72*, 1188–204.

Black, K. & Lobo, M. (2008). A conceptual review of family resilience factors. *Journal of Family Nursing, 14*, 33–55.

Bleil, M. E., McCaffery, J. M., Muldoon, M. F., Sutton-Tyrrell, K. & Manuck, S. B. (2004). Anger-related personality traits and carotid artery atherosclerosis in untreated hypertensive men. *Psychosomatic Medicine, 66*, 633–9.

Boyle, S. H., Williams, R. D., Mark, D. B., Brummett, B. H., Siegler, I. C., Helms, M. J., Barefoot, J. C. (2004). Hostility as a predictor of survival in patients with coronary heart disease. *Psychosomatic Medicine, 66*, 629–32.

Brach, E. L., Camara, K. A. & Houser, R. F. (2000). Patterns of interaction in divorced and non-divorced families: Conflict in dinnertime conversation. *Journal of Divorce and Remarriage, 33* (1–2), 75–89.

Bradbury, T. N. & Fincham, F. D. (1990). Attributions in marriage: Review and critique. *Psychological Bulletin, 107*, 3–33.

Bradford, K., Barber, B. K., Olsen, J. A., Maughan, S. L., Erickson, L. D., Ward, D. & Stolz, H. E. (2003). A multi-national study of interparental conflict, parenting, and adolescent functioning. *Marriage & Family Review, 35*, 107–37.

Braiker, H. B. & Kelley, H. H. (1979). Conflict in the development of close relationships. In R. L. Burgess & T. L. Huston (Eds.), *Social exchange in developing relationships* (pp. 135–68). New York: Academic Press.

Braithwaite, D. O. & Baxter, L. A. (2006). "You're my parent but you're not": Dialectical tensions in stepchildren's perceptions about communicating with the nonresidential parent. *Journal of Applied Communication Research, 34*, 30–48.

Braithwaite, D. O., Toller, P. W., Daas, K. L., Durham, W. T. & Jones, A. C. (2008). Centered but not caught in the middle: Stepchildren's perceptions of dialectical contradictions in the communication of co-parents. *Journal of Applied Communication Research, 36*, 33–55.

Branje, S. J., van Doorn, M., van der Valk, I. & Meeus, W. (2009). Parent–adolescent conflicts, conflict resolution types, and adolescent adjustment. *Journal of Applied Developmental Psychology, 30*, 195–204.

Bray, J. H. & Kelly, J. (1998). *Stepfamilies: Love, marriage, and parenting in the first decade.* New York: Broadway Books.

References

Brody, G. H. (1998). Sibling relationship quality: Its causes and consequences. *Annual Review of Psychology, 49*, 1–24.

Brody, G., Stoneman, Z., McCoy, J. K. & Forehand, R. (1992). Contemporaneous and longitudinal associations of sibling conflict with family relationship assessment and family discussions about sibling problems. *Child Development, 63*, 391–400.

Buchanan, C. M. & Heiges, K. L. (2001). When conflict continues after the marriage ends: Effects of postdivorce conflict on children. In J. H. Gyrch & F. D. Fincham (Eds.), *Interparental conflict and child development* (pp. 337–62). Cambridge: Cambridge University Press.

Buchanan, C. M., Maccoby, E. E. & Dornbasch, S. M. (1991). Caught between parents: Adolescents' experience in divorced homes. *Child Development, 62*, 1008–29.

Buehler, C. & Gerard, J. M. (2002). Marital conflict, ineffective parenting, and children's and adolescents' maladjustment. *Journal of Marriage and the Family, 84*, 78–92.

Bullock, B. M., Bank, L. & Burraston, B. (2002). Adult sibling expressed emotion and fellow sibling deviance: A new piece of the family process puzzle. *Journal of Family Psychology, 16*, 307–17.

Burmester, D. & Furman, W. (1990). Perception of sibling relationships during middle childhood and adolescence. *Child Development, 61*, 1387–98.

Burt, S. A., McGue, M., Krueger, R. F. & Iacono, W. G. (2005). How are parent–child conflict and childhood externalizing symptoms related over time? Results from a genetically informative cross-lagged study. *Development and Psychopathology, 17*, 145–65.

Burt, S. A., McGue, M., Iacono, W. G. & Krueger, R. F. (2006). Differential parent–child relationships and adolescent externalizing symptoms: Cross-lagged analyses within monozygotic twin differences design. *Developmental Psychology, 42*, 1289–98.

Buzzanell, P. M. (2010). Resilience: Talking, resisting, and imagining new normalcies into being. *Journal of Communication, 60*, 1–14.

Campione-Barr, N. & Smetana, J. G. (2010). "Who said you could wear my sweater?" Adolescent siblings' conflicts and associations with relationship quality. *Child Development, 81*, 464–71.

Canary, D. J. & Cupach, W. R. (1988). Relational and episodic characteristics associated with conflict tactics. *Journal of Social and Personal Relationships, 5*, 305–25.

Canary, D. J., Cupach, W. R. & Messman, S. J. (1995). *Relationship conflict: Conflict in parent–child, friendship, and romantic relationships*. Newbury Park, CA: Sage.

Canary, D. J. & Lakey, S., with Marmo, J. (2013). *Strategic conflict*. New York: Taylor & Francis/Routledge.

Canary, D. J., Stafford, L. & Semic, B. A. (2002). A panel study of the associations between maintenance strategies and relational characteristics. *Journal of Marriage and the Family, 64*, 395–406.

Canary, D. J., Weger, H., Jr. & Stafford, L. (1991). Couples' argument sequences and their associations with relational characteristics. *Western Journal of Speech Communication, 55*, 159–79.

Canary, H. E. (2008a). Creating supportive connections: A decade of research on support for families of children with disabilities. *Health Communication, 23*, 413–26.

Canary, H. E. (2008b). Negotiating dis/ability in families: Constructions and contradictions. *Journal of Applied Communication Research, 36*, 437–58.

Capaldi, D. M., Forgatch, M. S. & Crosby, L. (1994). Affective expression in family problem-solving discussions with adolescent boys. *Journal of Adolescent Research 9*, 28–49.

Cartwright, C. (2010). An exploratory investigation of parenting practices in stepfamilies. *New Zealand Journal of Psychology, 39*, 57–64.

Caughlin, J. P. & Huston, T. L. (2006). The affective structure of marriage. In A. L. Vangelisti & D. Perlman (Eds.), *The Cambridge handbook of personal relationships* (pp. 131–56). New York: Cambridge University Press.

Caughlin, J. P. & Malis, R. S. (2004). Demand/withdraw communication between parents and adolescents as a correlate of relational satisfaction. *Communication Reports, 17*, 59–71.

Caughlin, J. P. & Vangelisti, A. L (2000). An individual difference explanation of why married couples engage in demand/withdraw pattern of conflict. *Journal of Social and Personal Relationships, 17*, 523–51.

Caughlin, J. P. & Vangelisti, A. (2006). Conflict in dating and marital relationships. In J. G. Oetzel & S. Ting-Toomey (Eds.), *The Sage handbook of conflict communication: Integrating theory, research, and practice* (pp. 129–58). Thousand Oaks, CA: Sage.

Caughy, M. O., Huang, K.-Y. & Lima, J. (2009). Patterns of conflict interaction in mother–toddler dyads: Differences between depressed and non-depressed mothers. *Journal of Child & Family Studies, 18*, 10–20.

Cheng, C. C. (2010). A study of inter-cultural marital conflict and satisfaction in Taiwan. *International Journal of Intercultural Relations, 34*, 354–62.

Cheng, C. & Tardy, C. (2009). A cross-cultural study of silence in marital conflict. *China Media Research, 5*, 35–44.

Chesler, M. A. & Parry, C. (2001). Gender roles and/or styles in crisis: An integrative analysis of the experiences of fathers of children with cancer. *Qualitative Health Research, 11*, 363–84.

Choi, H. & Marks, N. F. (2008). Marital conflict, depressive symptoms, and functional impairment. *Journal of Marriage and the Family, 70*, 377–90.

Choi, Y., He, M. & Harachi, T. W. (2008). Intergenerational cultural dissonance, parent–child conflict and bonding, and youth problem behaviors among

Vietnamese and Cambodian immigrant families. *Journal of Youth and Adolescence, 37*, 85–96.

Christensen, A. & Heavey, C. L. (1990). Gender and social structure in the demand/withdraw pattern of marital conflict. *Journal of Personality and Social Psychology, 59*, 73–81.

Chuang, S. S. & Su, Y. (2009). Says who?: Decision-making and conflicts among Chinese-Canadian and mainland Chinese parents of young children. *Sex Roles, 60*, 527–36.

Cicognani, E. & Zani, B. (2010). Conflict styles and outcomes in families with adolescent children. *Social Development, 19*, 427–36.

Cinamon, R. G., Weisel, A. & Tzuk, K. (2007). Work–family conflict with the family: Crossover effects, perceived parent–child interaction quality, parental self-efficacy, and life role attributions. *Journal of Career Development, 34*, 79–100.

Clark, T. R. & Phares, V. (2004). Feelings in the family: Interparental conflict, anger, and expressiveness in families with older adolescents. *The Family Journal, 12*, 129–38.

Clarke, E., Preston, M., Raksin, J. & Bengtson, V. L. (1999). Types of conflict and tension between older parents and adult children. *The Gerontologist, 39*, 261–70.

Clements, M. L., Stanley, S. M. & Markman, H. J. (2004). Before they said "I do": Discriminating among marital outcomes over 13 years. *Journal of Marriage and Family, 66*, 613–24.

Coakley, R. M., Hombeck, G. N., Friedman, D., Greenley, R. N. & Thill, A. W. (2002). A longitudinal study of pubertal timing, parent–child conflict, and cohesion in families of young adolescents with spina bifida. *Journal of Pediatric Psychology, 27*, 461–73.

Cohen, S., Frank E., Doyle, W. J., Skinner, D. P., Rabin, B. S. & Gwaltney, J. M. (1998). Types of stressors that increase susceptibility to the common cold in healthy adults. *Health Psychology, 17*, 214–23.

Cole, A. K. & Kerns, K. A. (2001). Perceptions of sibling qualities and activities of early adolescents. *Journal of Early Adolescence, 21*, 204–26.

Coleman, M. A., Fine, M. A., Ganong, L. G., Downs, K. M. & Pauk, N. (2001). When you're not the Brady Bunch: Identifying perceived conflicts and resolution strategies in stepfamilies. *Personal Relationships, 8*, 55–73.

Collins, W. A. & Laursen, B. (1992). Conflict and relationships during adolescence. In C. U. Shantz & W. W. Hartup (Eds.), *Conflict in child and adolescent development* (pp. 216–41). New York: Cambridge University Press.

Cook, R. & DeFrain, J. (2005). Using discourse analysis to explore family strengths: A preliminary study. *Marriage & Family Review, 38*, 3–12.

Copstead, G. J., Lanzetta, C. N. & Avtgis, T. A. (2001). Adult children conflict control expectancies: Effects on aggressive communication toward parents. *Communication Research Reports, 18*, 75–83.

Crouter, A. C., Bumpus, M. F., Maguire, M. C. & McHale, S. M. (1999). Linking parents' work pressure and adolescents' well-being: Insights into dynamics in dual-earner families. *Developmental Psychology, 35*, 1453–61.

Courtright, J. A., Millar, F. E. & Rogers-Millar, L. E. (1979). Domineeringness and dominance: Replication and extension. *Communication Monographs, 46*, 179–92.

Crean, H. F. (2008). Conflict in the Latino parent–youth dyad: The role of emotional support from the opposite parent. *Journal of Family Psychology, 22*, 484–93.

Crockenberg, S. & Langrock, A. (2001). The role of specific emotions in children's responses to interparental conflict: A test of the model. *Journal of Family Psychology, 15*, 163–82.

Cue, M., Fincham, F. D. & Pasley, B. K. (2008). Young adult romantic relationships: The role of parent's marital problems and relationship efficacy. *Personality and Social Psychology Bulletin, 34*, 1226–35.

Cui, M. & Fincham, F. D. (2010). The differential effects of parental divorce and marital conflict on young adult romantic relationships. *Personal Relationships, 17*, 331–43.

Cummings, E. M. & Davies, P. T. (2010). *Marital conflict and children: An emotional security perspective.* New York: Guilford.

Cupach, W. R., Canary, D. J. & Spitzberg, B. H. (2010). *Competence in interpersonal conflict* (2nd edn). Long Grove, IL: Waveland.

da Silva, F. M., Jacob, E. & Nascimento, L. C. (2010). Impact of childhood cancer on parents' relationships: An integrative review. *Journal of Nursing Scholarship, 42*, 250–61.

Davies, P. T. & Cummings, E. M. (1998). Exploring children's emotional security as a mediator of the link between marital relations and child adjustment. *Child Development, 69*, 124–39.

DeBoard-Lucas, R. L., Fosco, G. M., Raynor, S. R. & Grych, J. H. (2010). Interparental conflict in context: Exploring relations between parenting processes and children's conflict appraisals. *Journal of Clinical Child and Adolescent Psychology, 39*, 163–75.

Deutsch, M. (1973). *The resolution of conflict: Constructive and destructive processes.* New Haven, CT: Yale University Press.

Diggs, R. C. & Socha, T. (2004). Communication, families, and exploring the boundaries of cultural diversity. In A. L. Vangelisti (Ed.), *Handbook of family communication* (pp. 249–66). Mahwah, NJ: Lawrence Erlbaum Associates.

Dix, T. H. (1991). The affective organization of parenting: Adaptive and maladaptive processes. *Psychological Bulletin, 110*, 3–25.

Dixon, S. V., Graber, J., A. & Brooks-Gunn, J. (2008). The roles of respect for parental authority and parenting practices in parent–child conflict among

References

African American, Latino, and European American families. *Journal of Family Psychology, 22,* 1–10.

Dorsey, S., Forehand, R. & Brody, G. (2007). Coparenting conflict and parenting behavior in economically disadvantaged single parent African American families: The role of maternal psychological distress. *Journal of Family Violence, 22,* 621–30.

Dotterer, A. M., Hoffman, L., Crouter, A. C. & McHale, S. M. (2008). A longitudinal examination of the bidirectional links between academic achievement and parent–adolescent conflict. *Journal of Family Issues, 29,* 762–79.

Dufur, M. J., Howell, N. C., Downey, D. B., Ainsworth, J. W. & Lapray, A. J. (2010). Sex differences in parenting behaviors in single-mother and single-father households. *Journal of Marriage and the Family, 72,* 1092–106.

Duggan, A. P. (2007). Sex differences in communicative attempts to curtail depression: An inconsistent nurturing as control perspective. *Western Journal of Communication, 71,* 114–35.

Duggan, A. P. & Le Poire, B. A. (2006). One down, two involved: An application and extension of inconsistent nurturing as control theory to couples including one depressed individual. *Communication Monographs, 73,* 379–405.

Dunn, J. (1983). Sibling relationships in early childhood. *Child Development, 54,* 787–811.

Dunn, J. & Munn, P. (1985). Becoming a family member: Family conflict and the development of social understanding. *Child Development, 56,* 480–92.

Dunn, J. D., Davies, L. C., O'Connor, T. G. & Sturgess, W. (2001). Family lives and friendships: Perspectives of kids in step-, single-parent, and non-step families. *Journal of Family Psychology, 15,* 272–87.

Du Rocher Schudlich, T. D. & Cummings, E. M. (2007). Parental dysphoria and children's adjustment: Marital conflict styles, children's emotional security, and parenting as mediators of risk. *Journal of Abnormal Child Psychology, 35,* 627–39.

Du Rocher Schudlich, T. D., Papp, L. M. & Cummings, E. M. (2004). Relations of husbands' and wives' dysphoria to marital conflict resolution strategies. *Journal of Family Psychology, 18,* 171–83.

Du Rocher Schudlich, T. D., Papp, L. M. & Cummings, E. M. (2011). Relations between spouses' depressive symptoms and marital conflict: A longitudinal investigation of the role of conflict resolution styles. *Journal of Family Psychology, 25,* 531–40.

Edwards, G., Barkley, R. A., Laneri, M., Fletcher, K. & Metevia, L. (2001). Parent–adolescent conflict in teenagers with ADHD and ODD. *Journal of Abnormal Child Psychology, 29,* 557–72.

Eisenberg, A. R. (1992). Conflicts between mothers and their young children. *Merrill-Palmer Quarterly, 38,* 21–43.

El-Sheikh, M. & Elmore-Staton, L. (2004). The link between marital conflict and child adjustment: Parent–child conflict and perceived attachments as mediators, potentiators, and mitigators of risk. *Development and Psychopathology*, 16, 631–48.

El-Sheikh, M. & Flanagan, E. (2001). Parental problem drinking and children's adjustment: Family conflict and parental depression as mediators and moderators of risk. *Journal of Abnormal Child Psychology*, 29, 417–32.

Fear, J. M., Champion, J. E., Reeslund, K. L., Forehand, R., Colletti, C., Roberts, L., et al. (2009). Parental depression and interparental conflict: Children and adolescents' self-blame and coping responses. *Journal of Family Psychology*, 23, 762–6.

Feinberg, M. E., McHale, S. M., Crouter, A. C. & Cumsville, P. (2003). Sibling differentiation: Sibling and parent relationship trajectories in adolescence. *Child Development*, 74, 1261–74.

Feldman, R., Masalha, S. & Derdikman-Eiron, R. (2010). Conflict resolution in the parent–child, marital, and peer contexts and children's aggression in the peer group: A process-oriented cultural perspective. *Developmental Psychology*, 46, 310–25.

Fine, M. A. (2001). Marital conflict in stepfamilies. In J. H. Grych & F. D. Fincham (Eds.), *Interparental conflict and child development: Theory, research, and application* (pp. 363–83). Cambridge: Cambridge University Press.

Fisher, B. A. (1978). *Perspectives on human communication*. New York: Macmillan.

Fitzpatrick, M. A. (1988). *Between husbands and wives: Communication in marriage*. Thousand Oaks, CA: Sage.

Flannery, D. J., Montemayor, R., Eberly, M. & Torquati, J. (1993). Unraveling the ties that bind: Affective expression and perceived conflict in parent adolescent interactions. *Journal of Social and Personal Relationships*, 10, 495–509.

Foote, R. C. & Holmes-Lonergan, H. A. (2003). Sibling conflict and theory of mind. *British Journal of Developmental Psychology*, 21, 45–58.

Fosco, G. M. & Grych, J. H. (2007). Emotional expression in the family as a context for children's appraisals of interparental conflict. *Journal of Family Psychology*, 21, 248–58.

Fosco, G. M. & Grych, J. H. (2010). Adolescent triangulation into parental conflicts: Longitudinal implications for appraisals and adolescent–parent relations. *Journal of Marriage and the Family*, 72, 234–66.

Frank, H. (2007). Young adults' relationships with parents and siblings: The role of marital status, conflict, and post-divorce predictors. *Journal of Marriage and the Family*, 46, 105–24.

Galovan, A. M., Fackrell, T., Buswell, L., Jones, B. L., Hill, E. J. & Carroll, S. J. (2010). The work–family interface in the United States and Singapore: Conflict across cultures. *Journal of Family Psychology*, 5, 646–56.

Gamble, W. C., Yu, J. J. & Kuehn, E. D. (2011). Adolescent sibling relationship quality and adjustment: Sibling trustworthiness and modeling as factors directly and indirectly influencing these associations. *Social Development, 20,* 605–23.

Ganong, L. H. & Coleman, M. (1993). A meta-analytic comparison of the self-esteem and behavioral problems of stepchildren to children in other family structures. *Journal of Divorce and Remarriage, 19,* 143–63.

Ganong, L. H. & Coleman, M. (2004). *Stepfamily relationships.* New York: Kluwer/Plenum.

Ganong, L. H., Coleman, M. & Hans, J. (2006). Divorce as prelude to stepfamily living and its consequences of redivorce. In M. A. Fine & J. H. Harvey (Eds.), *Handbook of divorce and relationship dissolution* (pp. 409–34). Mahwah, NJ: Lawrence Erlbaum Associates.

Garcia, M. M., Shaw, D. S., Winslow, E. B. & Yaggi, K. E. (2000). Destructive sibling conflict and the development of conduct problems in young boys. *Developmental Psychology, 36,* 44–53.

Ge, X., Natsuaki, M. N. & Conger, R. D. (2006). Trajectories of depressive symptoms and stressful life events among male and female adolescents in divorced and nondivorced families. *Development and Psychopathology, 18,* 253–73.

Gerhardt, C. A., Vannatta, K., McKellop, M. M., Zeller, M., Taylor, J., Passo, M., et al. (2003). Comparing parental distress, family functioning, and the role of social support for caregivers with and without a child with juvenile rheumatoid arthritis. *Journal of Pediatric Psychology, 28,* 5–15.

Gerhardt, C. A., Gutzwiller, J., Huiet, K. A., Fischer, S., Noll, R. B. & Vannatta, K. (2007). Parental adjustment to childhood cancer: A replication study. *Families, Systems & Health, 25,* 263–75.

Golish, T. D. (2003). Stepfamily communication strengths: Understanding the ties that bind. *Human Communication Research, 29,* 41–80.

Golish, T. D., and Caughlin, J. P. (2002). "I'd rather not talk about it": Adolescents' and young adults' use of topic avoidance in stepfamilies. *Journal of Applied Communication Research, 30,* 78–106.

Gottman, J. M. (1979). *Marital interaction: Experimental investigations.* New York: Academic Press.

Gottman, J. M. (1982). Emotional responsiveness in marital conversations. *Journal of Communication, 32,* 108–20.

Gottman, J. M. (1994). *What predicts divorce? The relationship between marital process and marital outcomes.* Hillsdale, NJ: Erlbaum.

Gottman, J. M. & Levenson, R. W. (2002). A two-factor model for predicting when a couple will divorce: Exploratory analyses using 14-year longitudinal data. *Family Process, 41,* 83–96.

Green, S. G., Bull Schaefer, R. A., MacDermid, S. M. & Weiss, H. M. (2011). Partner reactions to work-to-family conflict: Cognitive appraisal and indirect crossover in couples. *Journal of Management, 37,* 744–69.

Greenhaus, J. H. & Beutell, N. J. (1985). Sources and conflict between work and family roles. *Academy of Management Review, 10,* 76–88.

References

Grych, J. H. & Fincham, F. D. (1990). Marital conflict and children's adjustment: A cognitive-contextual framework. *Psychological Bulletin, 108*, 267–90.

Grych, J. H. & Fincham, F. D. (1993). Children's appraisals of marital conflict: Initial investigations of the cognitive-contextual framework. *Child Development, 64*, 215–30.

Grych, J. H., Raynor, S. R. & Fosco, G. M. (2004). Family processes that shape the impact of interparental conflict on adolescents. *Development and Psychopathology, 16*, 649–65.

Grzywacz, J. G. & Bass, B. L. (2003). Work, family, and mental health: Testing different models of work–family fit. *Journal of Marriage and Family, 65*, 248–62.

Guerrero, L. K., La Valley, A. G. & Farinelli, L. (2008). The experience and expression of anger, guilt, and sadness in marriage: An equity theory explanation. *Journal of Social and Personal Relationships, 25*, 699–724.

Hanson, T. L., McLanahan, S. S. & Thomson, E. (1996). Double jeopardy: Parental conflict and stepfamily outcomes for children. *Journal of Marriage and the Family, 58*, 141–54.

Harris, M. A., Antal, H., Oelbaum, R., Buckloh, L. M., White, N. H. & Wysocki, T. (2008). Good intentions gone awry: Assessing parental "miscarried helping" in diabetes. *Families, Systems, & Health, 26*, 393–403.

Hatfield, E., Traupmann, J., Sprecher, S., Utne, M. & Hay, M. (1985). Equity in close relationships. In W. Ickes (Ed.), *Compatible and incompatible relationships* (pp. 91–117). New York: Springer-Verlag.

Henne, E., Buysse, A. & Van Oost, P. (2007). An interpersonal perspective on depression: the role of marital adjustment, conflict communication, attributions and attachment within a clinical sample. *Family Process, 46*, 499–515.

Herzog, M. J. & Cooney, T. M. (2002). Parental divorce and perceptions of past interparental conflict: Influences on the communication of young adults. *Journal of Divorce and Remarriage, 36*(3–4),89–109.

Hetherington, E. M. (1989). Coping with family transition: Winners, losers, and survivors. *Child Development, 60*, 1–14.

Hetherington, E. M. & Jodl, K. (1994). Stepfamilies as settings for child development. In A. Booth & J. Dunn (Eds.), *Stepfamilies: Who benefits? Who does not?* (pp. 55–79). Hillsdale, NJ: Lawrence Erlbaum Associates.

Hill, E. J. (2005). Work–family facilitation and conflict, working fathers and mothers, work–family stressors and support. *Journal of Family Issues, 26*, 793–819.

Hilton, J. M. & Desrochers, S. (2000). The influence of economic strain, coping with roles, and parental control on the parenting of custodial single mothers and custodial single fathers. *Journal of Divorce and Remarriage, 33*, 55–76.

Houser, R., Daniels, J., D'Andrea, M. & Konstam, V. (1993). A systematic behaviorally based technique for resolving conflicts between adolescents and their single parents. *Child and Family Behavior Therapy, 15*, 17–31.

References

Howe, N., Rinaldi, C. M., Jennings, M. & Petrakos, H. (2002). "No! The lambs can stay out because they got cozies": Constructive and destructive sibling conflict, pretend play, and social understanding. *Child Development, 73,* 1460–73.

Howe, N., Fiorentino, L. M. & Gariépy, N. (2003). Sibling conflict in middle childhood: Influence of maternal context and mother–sibling interaction over four years. *Merrill-Palmer Quarterly, 49,* 183–208.

Huang, K.-Y., Teti, D. M., Caughy, M. O., Feldstein, S. & Genevro, J. (2007). Mother–child conflict interaction in the toddler years: Behavior patterns and correlates. *Journal of Child & Family Studies, 16,* 219–41.

Huang, Y.-H., Hammer, L. B., Neal, M. B. & Perrin, N. A. (2004). The relationship between work-to-family conflict and family-to-work conflict: A longitudinal study. *Journal of Family and Economic Issues, 25,* 79–100.

Hwang, W.-C. (2006). Acculturative family distancing: Theory, research, and clinical practice. *Psychotherapy: Theory, Research, Practice, Training, 43,* 397–409.

Jandasek, B., Holmbeck, G. N., DeLucia, C., Zebracki, K. & Friedman, D. (2009). Trajectories of family processes across the adolescent transition in youth with spina bifida. *Journal of Family Psychology, 23,* 726–38.

Jaquet, S. E. & Surra, C. A. (2001). Parental divorce and premarital couples: Commitment and other relationship characteristics. *Journal of Marriage and the Family, 63,* 627–38.

Jenkins, J. M. & Smith, M. A. (1991). Marital disharmony and children's behavior problems: Aspects of a poor marriage that affect children adversely. *Journal of Child Psychology and Psychiatry, 32,* 793–810.

Johnson, A. J., Wright, K. B., Craig, E. A., Gilchrist, E. S., Lane, L. T. & Haigh, M. H. (2008). A model for predicting stress levels and marital satisfaction for stepmothers utilizing a stress and coping approach. *Journal of Social and Personal Relationships, 25,* 119–42.

Kamp Dush, C. M. & Taylor, M. G. (2012). Trajectories of marital conflict across the life course: Predictors and interactions with marital happiness trajectories. *Journal of Family Issues, 33,* 341–68.

Kane, P. & Garber, J. (2004). The relations among depression in fathers, children's psychopathology, and father–child conflict: A meta-analysis. *Clinical Psychology Review, 24,* 339–60.

Kelley, D. L. (2012). *Marital communication.* Cambridge: Polity Press.

Kelly, A. B., Garnett, M. S., Attwood, T. & Peterson, C. (2008). Autism spectrum symptomatology in children: The impact of family and peer relationships. *Journal of Abnormal Child Psychology, 36,* 1069–81.

Kendall, J., Leo, M. C., Perrin, N. & Hatton, D. (2005). Modeling ADHD child and family relationships. *Western Journal of Nursing Research, 27,* 500–18.

Kiecolt-Glaser, J. K. & Newton, T. L. (2001). Marriage and health: His and hers. *Psychological Bulletin, 127,* 472–503.

References

Kiecolt-Glaser, J. K., Malarkey, W. B., Chee, M. A., Newton, T., Cacioppo, J. T., Mao, H. Y. & Glaser, R. (1993). Negative behavior during marital conflict is associated with immunological down-regulation. *Psychosomatic Medicine, 55,* 395–409.

Kiecolt-Glaser, J. K., McGuire, L., Robles, T. R. & Glaser, R. (2002). Psychoneuroimmunology: Psychological influences on immune function and health. *Journal of Consulting and Clinical Psychology, 70,* 537–47.

Kiecolt-Glaser, J. K., Gouin, J.-P. & Hantsoo, L. (2010). Close relationships, inflammation and health. *Neuroscience and Biobehavioral Reviews, 35,* 33–8.

Killoren, S. E., Thayer, S. M. & Updegraff, K. A. (2008). Conflict resolution between Mexican origin adolescent siblings. *Journal of Marriage and Family, 70,* 1200–12.

Kim, J.-Y., McHale, S., Osgood, D. W. & Crouter, A. C. (2006). Longitudinal course and family correlates of sibling relationships from childhood through adolescence. *Child Development, 77,* 1746–61.

Kinnunen, U., Feldt, T., Mauno, S. & Rantanen, J. (2010). Interface between work and family: A longitudinal individual and crossover perspective. *Journal of Occupational and Organizational Psychology, 83,* 119–37.

Kirby, E. L., Wieland, S. M. & McBride, M. C. (2006). Work/life conflict. In J. G. Oetzel & S. Ting-Toomey (Eds.), *The Sage handbook of conflict communication: Integrating theory, research, and practice* (pp. 327–57). Thousand Oaks, CA: Sage.

Koerner, A. F. & Fitzpatrick, M. A. (2006). Family conflict communication. In J. G. Oetzel & S. Ting-Toomey (Eds.), *The Sage handbook of conflict communication: Integrating theory, research, and practice* (pp. 159–83). Thousand Oaks, CA: Sage.

Kouros, C. D., Merrilees, C. E. & Cummings, E. M. (2008). Marital satisfaction and children's emotional security in the context of parental depression. *Journal of Marriage and the Family, 70,* 684–97.

Kramer, B. J., Kavanaugh, M., Trentham-Dietz, A., Walsh, M. & Yonker, J. A. (2009). Predictors of family conflict at the end of life: The experience of spouses and adult children of persons with lung cancer. *The Gerontologist, 50,* 215–25.

Kramer, L., Perozynski, L. A. & Chung, T. (1999). Parental responses to sibling conflict: The effects of development and parent gender. *Child Development, 70,* 1401–14.

Krishnakumar, A. & Buehler, C. (2000). Interparental conflict and parenting behaviors: A meta-analytic review. *Family Relations, 49,* 25–44.

Kurdek, L. A. (1991). Differences in ratings of children's adjustment by married mothers experiencing low marital conflict, married mothers experiencing high marital conflict, and divorced single mothers: A nationwide study. *Journal of Applied Developmental Psychology, 12,* 289–305.

Kurdek, L. A. & Fine, M. A. (1993). The relation between family structure and young adolescents' appraisals of family climate and parent behaviors. *Journal of Family Issues, 14,* 279–90.

Laible, D. J. & Thompson, R. A. (2002). Mother–child conflict in the toddler years: Lessons in emotion, morality, and relationships. *Child Development, 73,* 1187–203.

Laible, D., Panfile, T. & Makariev, D. (2008). The quality and frequency of mother–toddler conflict: Links with attachment and temperament. *Child Development, 79,* 426–43.

Lau, Y. K. (2010). The impact of fathers' work and family conflicts on children's self-esteem: The Hong Kong case. *Social Indicators Research, 95,* 363–76.

Laursen, B. (2005). Conflict between mothers and adolescents in single-mother, blended, and two-biological-parent families. *Parenting: Science and Practice, 5,* 347–70.

Laursen, B., Finkelstein, B. D. & Betts, N. T. (2001). A developmental meta-analysis of peer conflict resolution. *Developmental Review, 21,* 423–49.

Lavee, Y. & May-Dan, M. (2003). Patterns of change in marital relationships among parents of children with cancer. *Health & Social Work, 28,* 255–63.

Lee, S. S., Humphreys, K. L., Flory, K., Liu, R. & Glass, K. (2011). Prospective association of childhood attention-deficit/hyperactivity disorder (ADHD) and substance use and abuse/dependence: A meta-analytic review. *Clinical Psychology Review, 31,* 328–41.

Lockwood, R. L., Kitzmann, K. M. & Cohen, R. (2001). The impact of sibling warmth and conflict on children's social competence with peers. *Child Study Journal, 31,* 47–69.

Loving, T. J., Heffner, K. L., Kiecolt-Glaser, J. K., Glaser, R. & Malarkey, W. B. (2004). Stress hormone changes and marital conflict: Spouses' relative power makes a difference. *Journal of Marriage & Family, 66,* 595–612.

Ma, J. L. (2005). The diagnostic and therapeutic uses of family conflicts in a Chinese context: The case of anorexia nervosa. *Journal of Family Therapy, 27,* 24–42.

Ma, J. L. (2008). Eating disorders, parent–child conflicts, and family therapy in Shenzhen, China. *Qualitative Health Research, 18,* 803–10.

Maguire, K. C. (2012). *Stress and coping in families.* Cambridge: Polity.

Marmorstein, N. R. & Iacono, W. G. (2004). Major depression and conduct disorder in youth: Associations with parental psychopathology and parent–child conflict. *Journal of Child Psychology and Psychiatry, 45,* 377–86.

Marsh, D., Lefley, P., Evans-Rhodes, D., Ansell, V., Doerzbacher, B., LaBarbera, L., et al. (1996). The family experience of mental illness: Evidence for resilience. *Psychiatric Rehabilitation Journal, 20,* 3–12.

Matthews, R. A., Del Priore, R., Acitellie, L. K. & Barnes-Farrell, J. L. (2006). Work-to-relationship conflict: Crossover effects in dual-earner couples. *Journal of Occupational Health Psychology, 11,* 228–40.

McCubbin, M. & McCubbin, H. (1993). Family coping with health crises: The

References

resiliency model of family stress, adjustment and adaptation. In B. Danielson, B. Hamel-Bisell & P. Winstead-Fry, *Families, health, and illness* (pp. 3–63). St. Louis, MO: Mosby.

McCubbin, M. & McCubbin, H. (1996). Resiliency in families: A conceptual model of family adjustment and adaptation in response to stress and crisis. In H. McCubbin, A. Thompson & M. McCubbin (Eds.), *Family assessment: Resiliency, coping and adaptiation – inventories for research and practice* (pp. 1–64). Madison, WI: University of Wisconsin System.

McGuire, S., Manke, B., Eftekhari, A. & Dunn, J. (2000). Children's perceptions of sibling conflict during middle childhood: Issues and sibling (dis)similarity. *Social Development, 9*, 173–90.

McLoyd, V. C., Harper, C. I. & Copeland, N. L. (2001). Ethnic minority status, interparental conflict, and child adjustment. In J. H. Grych & F. D. Fincham (Eds.), *Interparental conflict and child development: Theory, research, and application* (pp. 98–125). New York: Cambridge University Press.

McLoyd, V., Toyokawa, T. & Kaplan, R. (2008). Work demands, work–family conflict, and child adjustment in African American families: The mediating role of family routines. *Journal of Family Issues, 29*, 1247–67.

Metz, M. E. & Epstein, N. (2002). Assessing the role of relationship conflict and in sexual dysfunction. *Journal of Sex and Marital Therapy, 28*, 139–64.

Mikami, A. Y. & Pfiffner, L. J. (2008). Sibling relationships among children with ADHD. *Journal of Attention Disorders, 11*, 482–92.

Mikkelson, A. C. (2006). Communication among peers: Adult sibling relationships. In K. Floyd & M. T. Morman (Eds.), *Widening the family circle: New research in family communication* (pp. 21–35). Thousand Oaks, CA: Sage.

Milevsky, A., Schlechter, M. J. & Machlev, M. (2011). Effects of parenting style and involvement in sibling conflict on adolescent sibling relationships. *Journal of Social and Personal Relationships, 28*, 1130–48.

Millar, F. & Rogers, L. E. (1976). Relational dimensions of interpersonal dynamics. In G. R. Miller (Ed.), *Explorations in interpersonal communication* (pp. 117–39). Newbury Park, CA: Sage.

Miller, G. E., Dopp, J. M., Myers, H. F., Stevens, S. Y. & Fahey, J. L. (1999). Psychosocial predictors of natural killer cell mobilization during marital conflict. *Health Psychology, 18*, 262–71.

Miller-Johnson, S., Emery, R. E., Marvin, R. S., Clarke, W., Lovinger, R. & Martin, M. (1994). Parent–child relationships and the management of insulin-dependent diabetes mellitus. *Journal of Consulting and Clinical Psychology, 62*, 603–10.

Montemayor, R. & Hanson, E. (1985). A naturalistic view of conflict between adolescents and their parents and siblings. *Journal of Early Adolescence, 5*, 23–30.

Morris, M. H. & West, C. (2001). Post-divorce conflict and avoidance of intimacy. *Journal of Divorce and Remarriage, 35*(3–4), 93–105.

References

Nixon, C. L. & Cummings, E. M. (1999). Sibling disability and children's reactivity to conflicts involving family members. *Journal of Family Psychology, 13,* 274–85.

Noller, P., Feeney, J. A., Bonnell, D. & Callan, V. J. (1994). A longitudinal study of conflict in early marriage. *Journal of Social and Personal Relationships, 11,* 233–52.

Noller, P., Feeney, J. A., Sheehan, G. & Peterson, C. (2000). Marital conflict patterns: Links with family conflict and family members' perceptions of one another. *Personal Relationships, 7,* 79–94.

O'Donnell, E. H., Moreau, M., Cardmeil, E. V. & Pollarsti, A. (2010). Interparental conflict, parenting, and childhood depression in a diverse urban population: The role of general cognitive style. *Journal of Youth Adolescence, 39,* 12–22.

Oetzel, J., Ting-Toomey, S., Chew-Sanchez, M. I., Harris, R., Wilcox, R. & Stumpf, S. (2003). Face and facework in conflicts with parents and siblings: A cross-cultural comparison of Germans, Japanese, Mexicans, and US Americans. *The Journal of Family Communication, 3,* 67–93.

Osborne, L. N. & Fincham, F. D. (1996). Marital conflict, parent–child relationships, and child adjustment: Does gender matter? *Developmental Psychology, 42,* 48–75.

Ostrov, J. M. & Bishop, C. M. (2008). Preschoolers' aggression and parent–child conflict: A multiinformant and multimethod study. *Journal of Experimental Child Psychology, 99,* 309–22.

Overbeek, G., Stattin, H., Vermulst, A., Ha, T. & Engels, R. C. (2007). Parent–child relationships, partner relationships, and emotional adjustment: A birth-to-maturity prospective study. *Developmental Psychology, 43,* 429–37.

Pai, A. L., Greenley, R. N., Lewandowski, A., Drotar, D., Youngstrom, E. & Peterson, C. C. (2007). A meta-analytic review of the influence of pediatric cancer on parent and family functioning. *Journal of Family Psychology, 21,* 407–15.

Papp, L. M., Kouros, C. D. & Cummings, E. M. (2010). Emotions in marital conflict interactions: Empathic accuracy, assumed similarity, and the moderating context of depression. *Journal of Social and Personal Relationships, 27,* 367–87.

Patterson, J. M. (2002). Integrating family resilience and family stress theory. *Journal of Marriage and Family, 64,* 349–60.

Paugh, A. & Izquierdo, C. (2009). Why is this a battle every night? Negotiating food and eating in American dinnertime interaction. *Journal of Linguistic Anthropology, 19,* 185–204.

Pawlowski, D. P., Myers, S. A. & Rocca, K. A. (2000). Relational messages in conflict situations among siblings. *Communication Research Reports, 17,* 271–7.

References

Perlman, M. & Ross, H. (2005). If-then contingencies in children's sibling conflicts. *Merrill-Palmer Quarterly, 51*, 42–66.

Perlman, M., Garfinkel, D. A. & Turrell, S. L. (2007). Parent and sibling influences on the quality of children's conflict behaviours across the preschool period. *Social Development, 16*, 619–41.

Phinney, J. S. (1986). The structure of 5-year-olds' verbal quarrels with peers and siblings. *The Journal of Genetic Psychology, 147*, 47–60.

Putnam, L. L. (2006). Definitions and approaches to conflict and communication. In J. G. Oetzel & S. Ting-Toomey (Eds.), *The Sage handbook of conflict communication: Integrating theory, research, and practice* (pp. 1–12). Thousand Oaks, CA: Sage.

Raffaelli, M. (1992). Sibling conflict in early adolescence. *Journal of Marriage and the Family, 54*, 652–63.

Raffaelli, M. (1997). Young adolescents' conflicts with siblings and friends. *Journal of Youth and Adolescence, 26*, 539–58.

Ram, A. & Ross, H. S. (2001). Problem solving, contention, and struggle: How siblings resolve a conflict of interests. *Child Development, 72*, 1710–22.

Ram, A. & Ross, H. S. (2008). "We got to figure it out": Information-sharing and siblings' negotiations of conflicts of interests. *Social Development, 17*, 512–27.

Randell, A. C. & Peterson, C. C. (2009). Affective qualities of sibling disputes, mothers' conflict attitudes, and children's theory of mind development. *Social Development, 18*, 857–74.

Raush, H. L., Barry, W. A., Hertel, R. J. & Swain, M. A. (1974). *Communication, conflict, and marriage*. San Francisco, CA: Jossey-Bass.

Recchia, H. E. & Howe, N. (2009a). When do siblings compromise? Associations with children's descriptions of conflict issues, culpability, and emotions. *Social Development, 19*, 838–57.

Recchia, H. E. & Howe, N. (2009b). Sibling relationship quality moderates the associations between parental interventions and siblings' independent conflict strategies and outcomes. *Journal of Family Psychology, 23*, 551–61.

Reese-Weber, M. (2000). Middle and late adolescents' conflict resolution skills with siblings: Associations with interparental and parent–adolescent conflict resolution. *Journal of Youth and Adolescence, 29*, 697–711.

Repetti, R. L. (1994). Short-term and long-term processes linking job stressors to father–child interaction. *Social Development, 3*, 1–15.

Repetti, R. L. & Wood, J. (1997). Effects of daily stress at work on mothers' interactions with preschoolers. *Journal of Family Psychology, 11*, 90–108.

Rhoades, K. A. (2008). Children's responses to interparental conflict: A meta-analysis. *Child Development, 79*, 1942–56.

Riggio, H. R. (2004). Parental marital conflict and divorce, parent–child relationships, social support, and relationship anxiety in young adulthood. *Personal Relationships, 11*, 99–114.

References

Rinaldi, C. M. & Howe, N. (1998). Siblings reports of conflict and the quality of their relationship. *Merrill-Palmer Quarterly, 44*, 404–22.

Rinaldi, C. M. & Howe, N. (2003). Perceptions of constructive and destructive conflict within and across family subsystems. *Infant and Child Development, 12*, 441–59.

Robin, A. L. & Foster, S. L. (1989). *Negotiating parent–adolescent conflict: A behavioral systems approach.* New York: Guilford.

Rogers, L. E. (2006). Relational communication theory: An interactional family theory. In D. O Braithwaite & L. A. Baxter (Eds.), *Engaging theories in family communication: Multiple perspectives* (pp. 115–29). Thousand Oaks, CA: Sage.

Rogers, L. E. & Farace, R. (1975). Analysis of relational communication in dyads: New measurement procedures. *Human Communication Research, 1*, 222–39.

Ross, H., Ross, M., Stein, N. & Trabasso, T. (2006). How siblings resolve their conflicts: The importance of first offers, planning, and limited opposition. *Child Development, 77*, 1730–45.

Sandhya, S. (2009). The social context of marital happiness in urban Indian couples: Interplay of intimacy and conflict. *Journal of Marital and Family Therapy, 35*, 74–96.

Scharlach, A., Li, W. & Dalvi, T. B. (2006). Family conflict as a mediator of caregiver strain. *Family Relations, 55*, 625–35.

Schermerhorn, A. C., Chow, S.-M. & Cummings, E. M. (2010). Developmental family processes and interparental conflict: Patterns of microlevel influences. *Developmental Psychology, 46*, 869–85.

Schmeeckle, M., Giarusso, R., Du, F. & Bengstom, V. L. (2006). What makes someone family? *Journal of Marriage and the Family, 68*, 595–610.

Schrodt, P. (2006). A typological examination of communication competence and mental health in stepchildren. *Communication Monographs, 73*, 309–33.

Schrodt, P. (2009). Family strength and satisfaction as functions of family communication environments. *Communication Quarterly, 57*, 171–86.

Schrodt, P. & Afifi, T. (2007). Communication processes that predict young adults' feelings of being caught and their associations with mental health and family satisfaction. *Communication Monographs, 74*, 200–28.

Schrodt, P., Soliz, J. & Braithwaite, D. O. (2008). A social relations model of everyday talk and relational satisfaction in stepfamilies. *Communication Monographs, 75*, 190–217.

Segrin, C. (2000). Social skills deficits associated with depression. *Clinical Psychology Review, 20*, 379–403.

Segrin, C. & Flora, J. (2005). *Family communication.* Mahwah, NJ: Lawrence Erlbaum.

Segrin, C. T., Melissa E. & Altman, J. (2005). Social cognitive mediators and relational outcomes associated with parental divorce. *Journal of Social and Personal Relationships, 22,* 361–77.

Selman, R. L. (1980). *The growth of interpersonal understanding: Developmental and clinical analyses.* New York: Academic Press.

Selman, R. L. (2003). *The promotion of social awareness: Powerful lessons from the partnership of developmental theory and classroom practice.* New York: Russell Sage Foundation.

Shamir, H., Cummings, E. M., Davies, P. T. & Goeke-Morey, M. C. (2005). Children's reactions to marital conflict in Israel and in the United States. *Parenting: Science and Practice, 5*(4), 71–86.

Shantz, C. U. & Hartup, W. W. (1992). Conflict and development: An introduction. In C. U. Shantz & W. W. Hartup (Eds.), *Conflict in child and adolescent development* (pp. 1–11). Cambridge: Cambridge University Press.

Shelton, K. H. & Harold, G. T. (2008). Interparental conflict, negative parenting, and children's adjustment: Bridging links between parents' depression and children's psychological distress. *Journal of Family Psychology, 22,* 712–24.

Sherman, A. M., Lansford, J. E. & Volling, B. L. (2006). Sibling relationships and best friendships in young adulthood: Warmth, conflict, and well-being. *Personal Relationships, 13,* 151–65.

Shimkowski, J. R. & Schrodt, P. (2012). Coparental communication as a mediator of interparental conflict and young adult children's mental well-being. *Communication Monographs, 79,* 48–71.

Siddiqui, A. A. & Ross, H. S. (1999). How do sibling conflicts end? *Early Education and Development, 10,* 315–32.

Siffert, A. & Schwarz, B. (2011). Spouses' demand and withdrawal during marital conflict in relation to their subjective well-being. *Journal of Social and Personal Relationships, 28,* 262–77.

Sillars, A. L. & Canary, D. J. (2013). Conflict and relational quality in families. In A. L. Vangelisti (Ed.), *Handbook of family communication* (2nd edn) (pp. 338–57). New York: Routledge.

Sillars, A. L., Canary, D. J. & Tafoya, M. A. (2004). Communication conflict and the quality of family relationships. In A. L. Vangelisti (Ed.), *Handbook of Family Communication.* Mahwah, NJ: Lawrence Erlbaum.

Sillars, A. L., Roberts, L. J., Leonard, K. E. & Dun, T. (2000), Cognition during marital conflict: The relationship of thought and talk. *Journal of Social and Personal Relationships, 1,* 479–502.

Sillars, A., Smith, T. & Koerner, A. (2010). Misattributions contributing to empathic (in)accuracy during parent–adolescent conflict discussions. *Journal of Social and Personal Relationships, 27,* 727–47.

Sillars, A. L. & Weisberg, J. (1987). Conflict as a social skill. In M. E. Roloff & G. R. Miller (Eds.), *Interpersonal processes: New directions in communication research* (pp. 140–71). Newbury Park, CA: Sage.

Sillars, A. L. & Wilmot, W. W. (1994). Communication strategies in conflict and

References

mediation. In J. A. Daly & J. M. Wiemann (Eds.), *Strategic interpersonal communication* (pp. 163–90). Hillsdale, NJ: Erlbaum.

Smetana, J. G. (1988). Adolescents' and parents' conceptions of parental authority. *Child Development, 59*, 321–35.

Smetana, J. G. (1989). Adolescents' and parents' reasoning about actual family conflict. *Child Development, 60*, 1052–67.

Smetana, J. G., Yau, J., Restrepo, A., Braeges, J. L. (1991). Adolescent–parent conflict in married and divorced families. *Developmental Psychology, 27*, 1000–10.

Smetana, J. G., Daddis, C. & Chuang, S. S. (2003). "Clean your room!" A longitudinal investigation of adolescent–parent conflict and conflict resolution in middle-class African American families. *Journal of Adolescent Research, 18*, 631–50.

Socha, T. J. & Yingling, J. (2010). *Families communicating with children.* Cambridge: Polity.

Spanos, A., Klump, K. L., Burt, S. A., McGue, M. & Iacono, W. G. (2010). A longitudinal investigation of the relationship between disordered eating attitudes and behaviors and parent–child conflict: A monozygotic twin differences design. *Journal of Abnormal Psychology, 119*, 293–9.

Sprecher, S. (2001). A comparison of emotional consequences of and changes in equity over time using global and domain-specific measures of equity. *Journal of Social and Personal Relationships, 18*, 477–501.

Sprey, J. (1971). On the management of conflict in families. *Journal of Marriage and the Family, 33*, 722–31.

Stafford, L. & Canary, D. J. (2006). Equity and interdependence as predictors of relational maintenance strategies. *Journal of Family Communication, 6*, 227–54.

Stocker, C. M., Lanthier, R. P. & Furman, W. (1997). Sibling relationships in early adulthood. *Journal of Family Psychology, 11*, 210–21.

Stocker, C. M., Burwell, R. A. & Briggs, M. L. (2002). Sibling conflict in middle childhood predicts children's adjustment in early adolescence. *Journal of Family Psychology, 16*, 50–7.

Stoneman, Z. (2001). Supporting positive sibling relationships during childhood. *Mental Retardation and Developmental Disabilities, 7*, 134–42.

Suarez, E. C. (2004). C-Reactive protein is associated with psychological risk factors of cardiovascular disease in apparently healthy adults. *Psychosomatic Medicine, 66*, 684–91.

Suarez, E. C., Kuhn, C. M., Schanberg, S. M., Williams, R. B., Jr. & Zimmermann, E. A. (1998). Neuroendocrine, cardiovascular, and emotional responses of hostile men: The role of interpersonal challenge. *Psychosomatic Medicine, 60*, 78–88.

Sullivan, K. T., Pasch, L. A., Johnson, M. D. & Bradbury, T. N. (2010). Social

References

support, problem solving, and the longitudinal course of marriage. *Journal of Personality and Social Psychology, 98,* 631–44.

Teachman, J., Tedrow, L. & Hall, M. (2006). The demographic future of divorce and dissolution. In M. A. Fine & J. H. Harvey (Eds.), *Handbook of divorce and relationship dissolution* (pp. 59–82). Mahwah, NJ: Lawrence Erlbaum Associates.

Ting-Toomey, S. (1983). An analysis of verbal communication patterns in high and low marital adjustment groups. *Human Communication Research, 9,* 306–19.

Tsai-Chae, A. H. & Nagata, D. K. (2008). Asian values and perceptions of intergenerational family conflict among Asian American students. *Cultural Diversity and Ethnic Minority Psychology, 14,* 205–14.

Umberson, D., Williams, K., Powers, D. A., Liu, H. & Needham, B. (2006). You make me sick: Marital quality and health over the life course. *Journal of Health and Social Behavior, 47,* 1–16.

United Nations Department of Economic and Social Affairs (2012). *Population facts No. 2012/1.* Population Division. Retrieved from http://www.un.org/esa/population/publications/popfacts/popfacts_2012-1.pdf

Updegraff, K. A., Thayer, S. M., Whiteman, S. D., Denning, D. J. & McHale, S. M. (2005). Relational aggression in adolescents' sibling relationships: Links to sibling and parent–adolescent relationship quality. *Family Relations, 54,* 373–85.

US Administration on Aging (2011). *Aging statistics.* Retrieved from http://www.aoa.gov/AoARoot/Aging_Statistics/index.aspx

US Census Bureau, Current Population Survey (2012). *Current population survey – definitions: Family.* Retrieved from http://www.census.gov/cps/about/cpsdef.html

Vandell, D. L. & Bailey, M. D. (1992). Conflicts between siblings. In C. U. Shantz & W. W. Hartup (Eds.), *Conflict in child and adolescent development* (pp. 242–69). New York: Cambridge University Press.

Van de Vliert, E. & Euwema, M. C. (1994). Agreeableness and activeness as components of conflict behaviors. *Journal of Personality and Social Psychology, 66,* 674–87.

Van Doorn, M. D., Branje, S. J. T. & Meeus, W. H. J. (2007). Longitudinal transmission of conflict resolution styles from marital relationships to adolescent–parent relationships. *Journal of Family Psychology, 21,* 426–34.

Van Yperen, N. W. & Buunk, B. (1990). A longitudinal study of equity and satisfaction in intimate relationships. *European Journal of Social Psychology, 20,* 287–309.

Vuchinich, S., Emery, R. E. & Cassidy, J. (1988). Family members as third parties in dyadic family conflict: Strategies, alliances, and outcomes. *Child Development, 59,* 1293–302.

References

Weaver, S. E. & Coleman, M. (2010). Caught in the middle: Mothers in step-families. *Journal of Social and Personal Relationships, 27,* 305–26.

Webster-Stratton, C. & Hammond, M. (1999). Marital conflict management skills, parenting style, and early-onset conduct problems: Processes and pathways. *Journal of Child Psychology and Psychiatry, 40,* 917–27.

Wheeler, L. A., Updegraff, K. A. & Thayer, S. M. (2010). Conflict resolution in Mexican-origin couples: Culture, gender, and marital quality. *Journal of Marriage and Family, 72,* 991–1005.

White, J. M. & Klein, D. M. (2008). *Family theories* (3rd edn). Thousand Oaks, CA: Sage.

Whitton, S. W., Olmos-Gallo, P. A., Stanley, S. M., Prado, L. M., Kline, G. H., St. Peters, M. & Markman, H. J. (2007). Depressive symptoms in early marriage: Predictions from relationship confidence and negative marital interaction. *Journal of Family Psychology, 21,* 297–306.

Wymbs, B. T. & Palham Jr., W. E. (2010). Child effects on communication between parents of youth with and without Attention-Deficit/Hyperactivity Disorder. *Journal of Abnormal Psychology, 119,* 366–75.

Yeh, K.-H. & Bedford, O. (2004). Filial belief and parent–child conflict. *International Journal of Psychology, 39,* 132–44.

Yu, T., Pettit, G. S., Lansford, J., Dodge, K. A. & Bates, J. E. (2010). The interactive effects of marital conflict and divorce on parent–adult children's relationships. *Journal of Marriage and Family, 72,* 282–92.

Zillman, D. (1993). Mental control of angry aggression. In D. M. Wegner & J. W. Pennebaker (Eds.), *Handbook of mental control* (pp. 370–92). Englewood Cliffs, NJ: Prentice-Hall.

Index